Voodoo through My Eyes

Belfazaar Ashantison

Design and Layout by Dark Moon Press

Published by Dark Moon Press

Copyright 2016

Voodoo through MY Eyes, Belfazaar Ashantison is published by
Dark Moon Press Ft. Wayne, Indiana

ISBN-13: 978-1537662824

For a full catalogue of Dark Moon's publications refer to

http://www.darkmoonpress.com

Or send an SASE to:

P.O. Box 11496, Ft. Wayne, Indiana, 46858-1496

Or send an SASE to:

Dark Moon Press

P.O. Box 11496, Fort Wayne, Indiana 46858-1496

Table of Contents

Preface

Asked to write anything on Voodoo/Vodou, one often encounters the whole "what SHOULD I write? What CAN I write?" and the "WHY should I write?" scenarios. There is a certain amount of secrecy that is necessary in a world that continues to struggle with what the true nature of something is and the need to pass down oral traditions to people who, in all reality, are caught up in the Jerry Springer-esque and Xbox/Play Station worlds. One struggles to keep things, entertaining, as well as, enlightening and informative without sounding all "oogie boogie" and "wrath of God". People tend, because of today's society, to have a lax sense of establishment and an ever shortening supply of attention.

When I was asked to do a book, by my own personal connection to Spirit, I truly thought, "How the hell am I supposed to pull this off without offending anyone?"… My connection to Spirit said, "You can't. Someone somewhere will always be offended by the actions you take, no matter your heart." And this statement is as true now, as it has been throughout history. There are generally TWO types of people who will spark up over a topic like this.

First, when the subject of a taboo nature makes its way to print, someone will always cry "FOUL!!!" and expect you to back down.

This, for the most part, is because of that whole "taboo" way of life where things, no matter how beautiful, or strong their connection to Spirit or how reverent they are to the Ancestors, will always have to stay partially in the shadows. Modern man simply doesn't WANT to dispel the ancient prejudices about issues as it gives them their reasons to continue to fear the things that go bump in the night.

Secondly, there is another class of people who will take offense to the fact that I am putting traditions to print. These are those people who will claim "cultural appropriation" as if no one can follow history and see that, at the core of each of the African Traditional Religion Offshoots (ATROs), there has been appropriations and collaborations to keep these LIVING traditions continuing to be viable in today's society. This is due to the fact that, even though they started off as belief systems working in harmony with the world around them, they have transformed into full fledged religions, complete with their own forms of dogmas and indoctrinations. Nor will they bother to understand that this has been my path for over TWO DECADES. This means that I LIVE, BREATHE, and even, WORK in and around my Voodoo Tradition. I still grow in knowledge, as I am also picking up more of the Haitian side of things with my current Godmothers, Mambo Maggie and her mother, Mama Lola. I am working on my initiation to become an Houngan (just an Houngan... I do not want to be Houngan Asogwe) and continuing to honor my Ancestors along the way.

This writing is sure to stir up mixed feelings in others as they have also done in me. To that, I can only state that what I put forth is my OWN understanding of the Voodoo tradition that I was blessed enough to be allowed to participate in and how it has effectively and collectively changed my life and set me on a path that was more in harmony with how my own heartfelt and the wishes that I strived daily to work towards. It has, for lack of a better way of putting it, made me a better man than I could have hoped to achieve without the practice. My original guide through Voodoo (New Orleans style), was an amazing woman who was taught by her Mother and Grandmother who were, in turn, taught by their Mothers and Grandmothers. She was a wonderfully talented, loving and caring woman who reminded me of my own Grandmother who helped raise me the majority of my life.

I was VERY blessed, indeed and have weighed out, very carefully, what I will and will not place in this book. "Voodoo Through My Eyes" is meant to be a "Voodoo 101" of a sort. It is meant to whet your appetite enough to learn about ANY of the African Traditional Religions (ATRs) and their offshoots, such as New Orleans style of Voodoo. So, please, disregard anything you might have heard or seen, such as the Hollywood attempts at portrayal of a system that they simply don't understand and have only an outsider's view of...

And I bid you... Welcome to "Voodoo through MY eyes"

A Quick Glossary

Every good book that I have ever truly enjoyed has shared one thing in common with each other. They contained a "glossary" for the terms used in the book. A basic way to pronounce things so that you could understand words that weren't exactly in the English vocabulary. I figured that I would add one here too.

Terms you will find in this book:

Aqwe: (ah gway) Agwe is the husband of the Haitian Loa, Lasirin and is the patron of anyone who makes their living on the seas and oceans. Be they navy, coast guard or fisherman, Agwe is going to work avidly to protect them and see that their livelihood is secure. He is also said to ferry the dead to the other side and protects travelers of all ilk.

Altar: (ahl tuhr) Altars are focal points of energy within the several magical systems. In New Orleans Voodoo tradition, the altar becomes the common core of the household communication to Ancestral Spirits, the Orisha, and the Loa.

Ashe: (ah SHAY) Ashe is a term that is both complex and elegantly simple at the same time. Ashe is considered the life force that can make things happen. It is that "spark" of God/Olodumare/Bondye that each of us carries to connect to the Creative Source. Ashe is used, in New Orleans Voodoo, as a greeting to other "practitioners" in much the same way as Namaste is used. It can also be used to add emphasis to a statement in a call and response sort of effort. Participants will either call back "ashe" or "ayebobo".

Ayebobo: (ah yee boh boh) Ayebobo is a term used to acknowledge the power of a statement. Ayebobo is used much the same way as "amen" is used to back a Preacher or Pastor in a church.

Baron Samedi: (bay won sahm dee) Baron Samedi is the Chief of the Ghede Spirits in the New Orleans Voodoo tradition. He is the guardian of the last crossroad you have to cross to become one with God/Olodumare/Bondye, husband of Mama Brigitte and father of Papa Ghede. When it is your time to cross over, Baron Samedi will guide you.

Bondye: (bon deeyeh) Bondye is the Haitian Kreyol for God, the Creator.

Chango/Shango/Xango: (shahn goh) Chango is the African Orisha associated with justice, male aspects of business, and associated with the primal forces of fire, thunder, and lightning.

Danballah & Ayedo Wedo: (dahn bah lah & ah yay doh way doh) An ancient duo of African Spirit who came to the America by way of the Haitian Vodou traditions. Representing the balance of nature and spirit, Danballah and Ayedo Wedo work in harmony to heal, spiritually cleanse and rebalance the scales.

Eleke: (eh lee keh) A necklace worn in many of the African Traditional Religions and their offshoots that are Orisha based and represents either the 7 primary African or a SPECIFIC Orisha, such as Chango or Ellegua.

Ellegua: (eh leh gwah) Ellegua is the African Orisha associated with the guarding the crossroads of life. Sought out in times of difficult decisions and correct choice, Ellegua is a force to be reckoned when it comes to the way roads can be opened or closed, making it easier for a person to travel forward in life or more difficult, should they need to learn a few extra lessons.

Erzulie Dantor: (ehr zoo lee dahn tohr) Erzulie Dantor is the patroness of single mothers and their children, women scorned by lovers, women in business (she has been seen in dreams dressed as a consummate business woman), and is a fierce warrior on behalf of those that seek her out.

Erzulie Freda: (ehr zoo lee fweh duh) Erzulie Freda is the sister of Erzulie Dantor and a patroness of those who seek love. Associated with attraction on all levels, she is also sought out the attraction of money, new jobs, and, even, new housing. Attraction on any level.

Erzulie Mapiyagn: (ehr zoo lee mah pee yahn) Erzulie Mapiyagn is the sister of Erzulie Dantor and Erzulie Freda. She is the patroness of the homeless and those with disabilities. She is sought out for people newly traumatized by disabilities to strengthen them for their long battle ahead as well as being the great protector of those who, through no fault of their own, have become homeless. This protector state also covers those who were thrown out of their homes for reasons they cannot control, such as unwanted children.

Ezili: (ee zee lee) Ezili is an ancient African Spirit, Orisha, associated with the moon, love, attraction, beauty, and women's mysteries. Ezili is rumored to be the progenitor of the Haitian Erzulie Spirits, however, most people disagree with this line of thought. This is one of the most important reasons that those that follow the New Orleans Voodoo tradition keep both the Orisha and Loa as SEPARATE beings.

Ghede (ghede): (geh deh) The Ghede (capital G) in New Orleans Voodoo watch out for all of the dead in New Orleans Voodoo (in Haitian Vodou, they watch out for the forgotten dead) and as such, they are the ones we go to in order to communicate with our Ancestors and fallen loved ones (ghede with a lower case g). When you really need some extra energy for your workings, go to the Ghede Spirits and ask them to bring your Ancestors together to aid you. There is a whole host of Spirits that identify in the Ghede family tree. Papa Ghede, Baron Samedi, Mama Brigitte, Baron Cemetrie (Cemetery), Baron Lacroix are among the many who work with and deal with our fallen loved ones.

Godmother/Godfather: In New Orleans traditional Voodoo, as well as other traditions, you have a person who takes you under their wing and teaches you the ways of Spirit. You fall under their tutelage throughout your tenure in the tradition, even upon reaching

16

the status of Priest or Priestess. It is through YOUR Godmother's or Godfather's guidance that you pick your godchildren.

Gris Gris: (gree gree) A Gris Gris is a charm bag filled with herb and root mixtures, blessed with oils and prayer work and then tied with chord or yarn. Conversely, during the early days of Voodoo in New Orleans, Gris Gris was also one of the terms used to hide 'magic'.

Juju: (joo joo) Juju, another term for 'magic', became a term associated with protective dolls.

Lasirin: (lah sih ren) Lasirin is an "Eternal Mother" Spirit, and as such, aids in the home and advancement of the home. She is sought to understand the deepest fathoms of the heart and soul and is said to rule over the bounties of the oceans.

Lave Tete: (lah veh teht) A Lave Tete is the initial initiation that a person receives from their Godmother or Godfather in the Voodoo tradition. It is to align a person with the spiritual power contained within the Voodoo tradition.

Mojo Hand: (moh joh hand) A mojo hand is another, more folk related, term for a Gris Gris bag. Mojo simply means 'magic'.

Obatala: (oh bah tah lah) Obatala is the African Orisha associated with the sky and the clouds. Linked to ancient wisdoms and deep knowledge, Obatala aids in scholastic endeavors and learning of any kind. Another Spirit associated with healing, spiritual cleansing, balance and renewal, Obatala works toward moving energies from a negative perspective to more positive perspective.

Ochosi: (oh choh see) Ochosi is the African Orisha associated with flora and fauna in the New Orleans tradition of Voodoo. He is a tracker and hunter and it is said that Ochosi's arrows can find the quickest way out of any situation… Not necessarily the smoothest and least painful, however, the quickest by far. Being linked to flora and fauna makes Ochosi an herbalist supreme. He can mix ANYTHING from the basics of healing to the most complex of poisons. He uses the knowledge to aid those that fall under his protection. Ochosi, like myself, is a protector and healer by nature.

Ogun: (oh goon) Ogun is the African Orisha associated with earth and metals in the New Orleans tradition of Voodoo. He is the one who taught us how to make tools, build farms, and even plant crops. This translates out to Ogun being the "Father of Technology" in today's Voodoo.

Olodumare: (oh loh doo mah reh) One of the African Traditional names for God, the Creator. It comes from the Yoruba traditions that heavily influenced the early stages of New Orleans traditions.

Oshun: (oh shoon) Oshun is the African Orisha associated with rivers, streams, and lakes. In New Orleans Voodoo, Oshun rules over the attraction of love and money, creative arts, and is even associated with "women's mysteries".

Oya: (oi yah) Oya is the African Orisha associated with change and transition in New Orleans Voodoo through her title as "Queen of the Winds and Hurricanes". As "Queen of the Market Place", she rules over business and, especially, women in business. As "Queen of the Cemeteries", Oya is our ultimate connection to our Ancestors. Oya is also the "Mother of Memory", as well, and as such, she aids in scholastic endeavors.

Paristyle: (payr ih steel) A paristyle is a temple where Voodoo practitioners gather to perform mutual ceremonies and is a term adopted from the Haitian Vodou traditions incorporated into the New Orleans Voodoo tradition.

Poto Mitan: (poh toh mee tahn) During ceremonies, inside or out, you can find practitioners dancing around a pole or tree that represents the center of the ceremony space. This central post, poto mitan, becomes the connection to the "World of Spirit", as my Godmother used to say.

Veve: (vay vay) A veve is a Haitian sigil that is a symbol of communication with specific Loa within the Haitian pantheon of Spirits during times of ceremony and can even be found on home altars to better stabilize the connection individuals and families have with those Spirits.

Yemaya: (yeh may yah) Yemaya is the African Orisha associated with motherhood, the hearth and home. She is associated, as well, with fertility and, as such, is often sought out to aid in having children. Yemaya also represents the bounty of the seas and oceans.

There's a saying in New Orleans Voodoo... "The Baron walk 'round here like nobody's business."

Veve for Ogou Badagris

 I figured that I would write this piece about New Orleans style of Voodoo to give people a better perspective of the path that I travel and perhaps a deeper understanding of just why I travel this path. I can only present this as the Tao of Zaar, the truth of Zaar, according to my own perspective and understanding of the New Orleans Voodoo that I was taught and hope that others following similar paths will find it informative and educational and that people, who may not have a path as of yet, will find it interesting and intriguing…

For those of you who don't know, New Orleans style of Voodoo is a combinative belief system. Beginning with a host of African Traditional Religions (ATRs), heavy with the influences of the Yoruban Traditions, brought over to the Western Hemisphere by way of the Caribbean Trade Route. It also combines elements found in and around the New Orleans area. These things include, but are not limited to, Catholicism/Christianity, European Religious Traditions (mostly in the form of tools that were incorporated in) and Native American customs and herbal knowledge (because when the Africans were ripped from their homelands, they had to be taught about herbs that would suffice to make the herbal remedies they had always used before). What makes this a truly eloquent system is that, it has been said , even, the original traditions, such as Ifa, believed that they never held the whole truth of God, therefore any time it finds a piece of the truth, it is incorporated into the system as a whole... And it is almost telegenic in nature. Meaning, when one system picks up a piece of the truth, it almost always travels back the line, resets the system and travels back outward to OTHER offshoots of the original traditions. A good example of this can be found in the form of the New Orleans Voodoo Doll. Houses/Families just didn't automatically pick it up overnight. It became a tried and tested product before spreading to other Houses/Families.

Picture it, if you will... A **LIVING** system of belief that allows for continued growth and renewal.

Make no mistake. New Orleans traditional Voodoo is its own entity entirely and should not be confused with Louisiana Voodoo (sometimes called Plantation Voodoo) or Haitian Vodou. Each of these traditions are living, breathing, and working systems contained within the Louisiana area.

There are differences between the systems that are VERY distinct. Louisiana Voodoo deals primarily with the Orisha and is more closely related to systems such as Santeria and Candomble in many cases. Haitian Vodou deals primarily with the Loa (also spelled Lwa), a group of Spirits that came to the forefront of the Spiritual realm during a time of great need for the Haitian slaves. And then you have New Orleans own tradition. New Orleans traditional Voodoo is a luscious blend of both the African Orisha and the Haitian Loa. Each set of Spirit Forces are given respect, entreated for daily blessings and honored with one major difference. In New Orleans it becomes a more fluid system with rituals flowing in a, somewhat, non-sequential manner. This is not to say that we don't do things such as start off with honoring and pouring libations for Ellegua and Papa Legba, this just means that we do not presume to dictate to Spirit what order they may come into our ceremonies to pass their messages.

Indeed... Some of our ceremonies may see Papa Legba, Ogun, Papa Legba again, a Ghede Spirit and even more come bounding through bringing messages of hope and healing, do workings of love,

Spiritual Cleansing or tell a person some message that they need to hear.

Here, in New Orleans, there are several legends about how it remained hidden and most of them agree on one thing… The easiest way to hide it was to NOT SPEAK OF IT. Instead, it was hinted at and new words were used/created to disguise the fact that someone was about to do magick on someone.

"I gots ta go play a *trick* on someone", "I gots my *mojo* brewin", "Woohie, I got to get my *juju* warmed up."

Phrases of this ilk became a standard for going to do a magickal working, yet there was an even more silent way of doing things… People just did it and still do in many ways… Here, as well, many people do things because Grandma and Great Grandma did them and they seemed to work really well. Examples are tossing salt out the doors, sprinkling red brick dust to ward off ill intent, three pennies at a crossroad to help win a decision and so forth became STANDARD in New Orleans culture without even mentioning where it came from nor who brought it with them. It literally became a background fixture in the culture… An indigenous piece of the scenery that was truly backed by a belief system that is constantly growing; constantly changing…

Veve for Mama Brigit

Throughout the course of the initial years of New Orleans tradition, we only dealt with the Orisha, the African Spirit Forces. These forces are almost always linked to some sort of natural phenomena. For an example, I will use the 7 Primary African Powers as listed in the book "Jambalaya" (Luisah Teish, HarperCollins) and represented by Voodoo Authentica (www.voodooshop.com) with a couple of others thrown in because this is also what my FIRST "Godmother" in Voodoo (though we all only called her Mama Anna Marie) taught me:

Ellegua = Sun

Obatala= Clouds and Sky

Chango= Fire, Lightning and Thunder

Oya= Winds and Hurricanes

Ogun= Earth and Metals

Yemaya= Seas and Oceans

Oshun= Creeks, Streams and Rivers

Ezili= Moon

Ochosi= Flora and Fauna

These Spirit Forces, all aligned under ONE CREATOR GOD, move through our lives on a daily basis. Each has his or her own sphere of influence and, though some of them may cross, work towards the Voodooist's/Vodouisant's betterment.

It wasn't until the 1800s and the advent of the Haitian Revolution (1791-1804) that New Orleans received the Loa and their particular blessings... The difference was almost immediately noticeable... The Haitian Loa, though having similar responsibilities and functions in our daily lives, have been more personified... Papa Legba, Mama Ayizan, Papa Danballah, Mama Dantor, Papa Ghede, Mama Brigit, Baron Samedi... The Spirit Forces from the ATRs shifted, once again, into LIVING representations of themselves. Just as they did in Africa, they once more walked among the people who were stripped from their homeland.

Remember, also, that things shifted when they came to the Western Hemisphere. Much knowledge was lost and people attempted, as best they could, to recreate and hold on to the information through memory, tales, songs and remembered rituals.

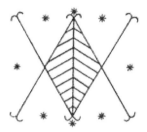

Veve for Mama Ayizan

There are literally HUNDREDS of Orisha and Loa to choose from, so in the effort to keep this simple, I will stop at listing these ones for now, as I plan on going into more detail about the Orisha and the Loa later in this writing. I just wanted to show you the difference between the Haitian Loa and the African Orisha... Ellegua and Papa Legba STILL act as the door openers. They still aid in decision making and communications issues. They still go to bat for you as Warrior Spirits. One is more akin to the Primal Forces which they sprang from, while the other is more personified and easily identifiable in our miniscule minds...

Make no mistake. Ellegua is an Orisha and Papa Legba is a Loa. They are two completely different beings who share similar capabilities and qualities... Though many practitioners may hold them on the same altar, we KNOW they are not the same being.

Just as in many belief systems, our human minds are fragile, at best, and cannot comprehend the whole truth of God/Olodumare/Bondye/Bondje. The absolute VASTNESS that is the Creative Source. The major truth about Voodoo/Vodou though, isn't the fact that it is a LIVING belief system that constantly grows and slowly changes. It is that it is, at its core, understanding of the fact that it never held the whole truth of God, so EACH time it finds a piece of that truth, no matter how miniscule that piece may be, it incorporates it and... Due to the living nature it continues to grow with each piece of truth that it finds. My first Godmother was fond of saying, "keep your eyes open, you never know what God is bringing your way."

This process of induction, flowing back to the roots of New Orleans traditions and spreading outward again aids in the perpetual growth and renewal of the systems that have evolved from the original ATRs. One of our most famous of all of these inductions is the European poppet. Though, admittedly, there are things very akin to them in SOME of the African Traditions, the Voodoo Doll IS our incorporation of the European poppet. When we first incorporated it into New Orleans style of Voodoo, it was used merely as a tool of identification and record keeping.

Example: During a particularly nasty time in our history, when indentured servants were being treated almost as brutally as our African slave population, these practitioners of the old craft turned towards the African spirituality to find solace. In working with African slaves, the indentured servants shared some of their own rich traditions and rites… One of these traditions was the making of a "poppet" to symbolize the person you were doing work for or on.

Thus, the Voodoo doll was born. Over the years, with practice, usage and focusing, we learned that we could use them as a focal tool that did not need for the person to be present for us to do our work. In cases such as this, when a person was too severely injured to be taken anywhere, others would then bring bits of your clothing you wore in whatever accident took place, bits of your nail trimmings and hair clippings. These would then be worked into the doll, along with the herbs, oils, roots and prayer work to, once again, effect a healing. The more severe the injury, the more pins would be found in the doll, marking EVERY place we were attempting to shuttle healing energy too.

Because Voodoo is a LIVING belief system, it evolves differently from house to house, practitioner to practitioner. There are SOME things that will ALWAYS be the same yet there are many more things that will differ in major ways… Understand that it is how you were taught to treat Spirit that will show through your actions in serving Spirit.

Marie Laveau

Marie Laveau, known better as the Voodoo Queen of New Orleans or the Widow Paris, was believed to be born September 10, 1794 and reputed to have died on June 15, 1881. A free woman of color, Marie Laveau was an influential force in New Orleans Voodoo practices. She was also what was called a Quadroon (born of African, Spanish, French, and Native American blood). What people fail to realize is that Marie was a devout Catholic and would attend services, if you will pardon the pun, religiously.

It was said that her RELIGION was Catholicism and her PRACTICE was Voodoo.

During her reign as "Voodoo Queen", Marie showed herself to be a true tour de force in her protection of her practicing family. She fought long and hard to make headways for both the People of Color and Voodoo practitioners alike. Legend has it that Marie Laveau made a deal with Pere Antoine, the Priest of St Louis Cathedral. The deal went something like this:

Marie Laveau approached the Priest of St Louis Cathedral, Pere Antoine, and spoke to him. "If you allow us to practice in piece, I will insure that the pews of the Cathedral are full." Pere Antoine, after much thought and prayer, returned to Marie Laveau and agreed to the bargain. Our families were allowed to practice their ways, while Catholic attendance rose in the St Louis Cathedral. To this day, the bargain that Marie Laveau laid out with Pere Antoine is in full effect.

Marie Laveau worked as a caregiver during times of yellow and scarlet fever outbreaks in the hospices and hospitals of 1800s Louisiana. Her ministering to the sick was not a walk she took alone. Marie was often seen in the company of Pere Antoine.

In her time, Marie was also a noted hairdresser. As with many hairdressers, Marie was privy to knowledge and gossip of the time. The consummate business woman, she would use this knowledge and gossip to acquire new clientele and provide work for people. She was also known as a "procuress". This means that Marie Laveau was sought out by people far and wide to "procure" things for them. If the person needed special herbs, Marie may traverse the swamps. If the person needed a marriage partner, she would even find them one of those. Often times buying these people out of slavery to wed. so, depending on which side of the slave trade you were on, she could be seen as either famous or infamous. (Personally, I consider her famous. Anyone who worked so hard to free people during an infamous time in American history, I would consider famous. That's just how I roll.)

Due to her prowess with Voodoo, Marie's history is still shrouded in myth and legend though writers, such as Dr Ina Fandrich, Martha Ward, and Carolyn Morrow Long, have endeavored to shine light into the passage of time and inform of us of how courageous a woman she really was.

For those who don't know:

Dr Ina Fandrich wrote the book *Marie Laveau the Mysterious Voodoo Queen*

Martha Ward wrote the book *Voodoo Queen: The Spirited Lives of Marie Laveau*

Carolyn Morrow Long wrote the book *A New Orleans Voudou Priestess; the Legend and Reality of Marie Laveau*

Both of the latter books acknowledge Dr Fandrich's work. Each have their own spin on Marie Laveau and tell the tale with subtle differences. Check them out for yourselves.

On the New Orleans Voodoo side of things, Marie Laveau is considered an "Elevated Spirit" and, to this day, still sought out to perform works. People visit her tomb in New Orleans at St Louis #1, leaving offerings and making requests of her and her power. There is a XXX (three X) ritual that is suggested to go along with requesting things from Marie Laveau. Be sure to visit Voodoo Authentica, at 612 Dumaine, right in the heart of the French Quarter and check out the instructions on the XXX ritual. Be sure to pay proper respects entering and exiting the cemetery, so as not to upset the ancestors.

When praying to Marie Laveau, my Voodoo family uses this particular prayer.

Marie Laveau Prayer

Benevolent Marie Laveau

Who draws her strength from the Orisha and God above

First in your prevailing love

And strengthening power

In your kindness

Give me the fortitude to

Confront the misfortunes I meet

With strength and grace

Confront the opportunities I meet

With love and humility

And the strength to overcome my weakness

"That is NOT what we're about"

I figured this next section should be about what is **NOT** Voodoo... In an effort to lay some very stereotypical and malicious thoughts and perceptions, preconceived notions and proselytized views to rest, I will be going through some commonly asked questions by some of the people who I've come across in my time as a practitioner of New Orleans style of Voodoo and a Voodoo Priest in New Orleans.

Question: Isn't Voodoo just another form of Devil worship?

Answer: No. Voodoo has nothing to do with the Christian concept of one Supreme Being of evil. There is no Lucifer/Satan/Devil. We do acknowledge that there are spirits dedicated to love and hate, good and ill will, "right" and "wrong" however; in Voodoo we don't name our negative energies. "To name something is to grant it power over you" thus we tend to ONLY name the good influences in our lives. We are NOT about to grant power over us to something we believe to be of a negative nature. It is just not our way.

Question: Isn't Voodoo a form of black magick?

Answer: No. Voodoo acknowledges Divine Magicks (magicks wrought by God/Olodumare/Bondye) however, magick, in and of itself, is neither black nor white. It is neither good NOR evil. It is, as with many of the natural things in life, neutral in nature. It can be used for good or ill and it is all in the intent of the user. Face it folks, there are good and bad people in EVERY religion on the face of the planet. Christian televangelists have bilked people out of MILLIONS of dollars. Priests have molested children. Wiccan Priestesses have forced marriages apart for the sake of a fling on the side. I can list off more. It runs in EVERY aspect of belief on the face of the planet... If there is a faith, someone will endeavor to use it to better their lives by making others suffer through their indulgences.

Magick is a force of nature and like many of those forces; it can cause good or bad based on the intention of the user. Like the fire that cooks your food and heats your home, in the hands of the arsonist, it can burn your home and belongs to cinders. Magick is a part of the natural world and has ALWAYS been so

In reality, many of the nation traditions, such as Ifa, did not have a form of "curse/hex" until it came to the western hemisphere... Something about the way that they were treated during and, more often than not, tricked into slavery devolved a system more than 7,000 years old into back water happenings and rumors of dark magicks and mysteries. Then again, if you were yanked from your homeland, forced into a completely different religion, lifestyle and mode of life, being treated as if you were a LESSER being, I bet YOU would change how you looked at things as well. Forced into less than second class citizenship; to live in squalor; to be subservient… These things would make any of us rethink how we looked at the world around us and the people within it.

Question: How can I force someone to love me and only me?

Answer: You can't. If the love wasn't there in the first place, it will probably never be there even with the installation of magicks. One question I always ask when a person speaks on doing this sort of magick is, "Do you want the person to fall in love with you or the magick?"

I ask this question of people for a reason. Any time that love is "forced" into a situation, it suppresses a person's free will for a time. Like ANY magick that is forced into a person, it runs its course eventually and when that person's free will reasserts itself, the "love" that was placed their flips to something much more heinous. Either the person becomes completely enraged and filled with hate towards the one who placed, or had placed, the "love magick" in them OR it becomes a form of deadly obsession causing the most nightmarish stalker situation a person can possibly think about. Because the love was never truly there and was forcibly placed in a person through magick, it eventually twists into its darker form.

In reality, there are several spells/tricks/conjures in Voodoo that can draw your true love to you, the trouble is… Is it going to be the person you have your eyes and heart set on? That being said, what do you do when you find out the person of your dreams is NOT who you have your eyes and heart set on? Do you tell God, "That isn't who I want"? Do you reject what God is presenting you like some spoiled brat who thinks that they know better than the Creator who is supposed to be with you?

If you can do this, you are a definitely ballsier than I… I would NEVER presume to tell God what he can and cannot do for me, who he can and cannot choose for me or what I will and will not accept from God…

Question: How many Gods are there in Voodoo?

Answer: Just one. By those in American practices, we call him simply God however, depending on how you were trained, who you were trained by and which tradition they primarily followed, God could be called Olodumare (from more African based traditions) or Bondye (from more Haitian based traditions)… My Godmother on the Haitian side of things, Mama Lola, and her daughter, Mambo Maggie have told me several times, "One God, many faces"… Literally this translates out to "everyone sees God as what they NEED to see Him" and that they call him how they see him too… If you see him from a more traditional Haitian side of things, you will often use "God" and "Bondye" interchangeably… Likewise, from the African side, "God" and "Olodumare" will cross your lips, mind and heart…

There are deified Spirits throughout all of the systems. These deified Spirits can honestly be called Voodoo Gods, however, most practitioners simply call them Orisha or Loa to distinguish them

38

from the Creative Source that is God/Olodumare/Bondye/Bondje. We attempt to make it VERY clear that there is ONLY ONE Creator God. The other Spirits are those that God grants power to in order to help us oversee our daily lives.

Question: How can I get revenge on this person for doing me wrong?

Answer: Like the old saying goes, "he who sets his heart on revenge should dig TWO graves." There is an old saying in Voodoo, "Nothing is done without the eyes of God"... This is to remind us that we ARE being watched and that God will call it out on us in the end, so be careful what you do to one another. This does not stop people from seeking vengeance for whatever perceived or real wrongs have been done to them; it just keeps those of us who WISH to remain in the healing, prosperity and protection side of the workings from straying from our callings. As I mentioned earlier, there are good people and bad people in EVERY religion on the face of the planet... Indeed... The very act of creating a religion seems to bring the sides out in a major way. Those who seek to help in whatever capacity they can. Those who seek to subjugate and enslave to serve their own indulgences... This is one of the primary reasons I don't really consider Voodoo, especially with the fluidity of New Orleans Voodoo, a religion. I consider it a Spiritual Path. There isn't really the whole dogma and indoctrination process that goes along with many other religions and it is fluid in its flow. Even though there are certain things that will ALWAYS happen and always take place, there is an ebb and flow that is PURELY New Orleans style Voodoo, as opposed to Haitian Vodou or even African Ifa…

Question: Can't I just get a Voodoo Doll and cause the person pain?

Answer: This is a loaded question from start to finish. Most people who are asking it are basing their interpretation of what Voodoo is by the myriad of Hollywood tales spun to intrigue us and relieve us of our hard earned money for a timely little distraction from our day to day grind. Others who are asking ARE seeking to harm another for whatever reason, most of which seems to revolve around some issue of jealousy in one way, shape or fashion.

Remember that, like any other icon of faith, the Voodoo Doll is merely a focal tool allowing magicks of a sympathetic nature to take place. By this, I mean that the magicks placed on the doll are meant to represent being placed on the person the doll is supposed to be a stand in for. This means that in order for it to truly be effective, like any other icon, YOUR faith plays the biggest part in the spell work being done. The more faith you have, the better the outcome… Unless it is something that Olodumare simply is telling you, "No. This will not be done to this person." In all things Voodoo, God/Olodumare/Bondye has the final say on whether it will come to pass or not.

Can negative forms of magick be done in this capacity? Of course, as I said earlier, there are good and bad people in EVERY religion on the face of the planet... Voodoo is no different. People come to the path for a myriad of reasons... Some of those people come to seek power over others by means of harming them when and where they would like. HOWEVER... Like every other faith based movement on the planet, your target would have to share a belief in the practice on some basic level in order for it to be effective and let us be completely truthful... There aren't an awful lot of people in the world that DO believe in systems that they haven't personally grown up with... Voodoo and many of the offshoots of the ATRs run into situations like this all the time.

Question: Where did Catholicism come into Voodoo?

Answer: During the 15th through 19th centuries and with the advent of slavery, the African Traditional Religions became the target of "forced conversion"... By this, I mean that the slavers of the time, predominantly being Catholic, told the African peoples that they had tricked, trapped and caged, "You will be Catholic or you will die...." There was no, "Well... C'mon we worship one God too! Why don't you make the switch???" No. This was forced onto a people who were no longer allowed to have their own homes, their own music, their own religion... In a sense, they were dehumanized to be used as nothing more than a pack animal/subservient being/slave...

**A whole treatise can be written about the treatment of the African slaves ripped from their homeland through trickery and outright

41

inhumanity however, I am not the one to write that story. I am merely a hand-picked servant of the Orisha and Loa working to bring a modicum of understanding to New Orleans Voodoo.**

Originally however, the practitioners of Voodoo hid behind Catholicism. By this, I mean that they took a serious look into Catholicism and found several like spirits in it with which they linked their own spiritual forces to. Altars were made and images of these newly synched spiritual forces attached to the altars thus creating a new way to identify with THEIR spiritual forces while maintaining the guise of being the "good little Catholic" for their overseers...

Remember though... Some of the root traditions believe that they never held the whole truth of God. This being the case, when Catholicism began to promote some truth, it became so intertwined within Voodoo that you can no longer separate the two pieces from the whole... They are now part and parcel of a living system that continually learns, adapts and grows all the while maintaining its roots...

And one that I have been asked on several occasions, personally...

Question: Why are YOU on THIS path?

Answer: From time to time, in one of the groups pertaining to African Spirituality that I am in, you find the same question being asked over and over again. Inevitably, this leads to a whole slew of racially charged arguments however, I thought I would take a different tack than my usual "club racism until it is dead" attitude that I am more normally known for.

The question, with my own twist, usually ends up being something along the lines of, "Why are there so many light skinned people in an African based Spirituality?"

I can't answer for anyone else save me, so I won't pretend to. I will however, share with you MY reasons for being in this path. Whether you like it or not, it is exactly that… MY path.

From an early age, it was clear that I could never fit God into that small box that so many others from my family seemed comfortable placing him in. I could never ascribe traits that were, most assuredly, "human" in nature to a "Supreme being of love and compassion"… Such as discrimination… I could also not picture the "Supreme being of love and compassion" being some bald, white guy with a big stick, sitting in the clouds, waiting to thump us should we ever do any wrong… It just didn't seem right, to me. Like something was missing PURPOSELY from what we were being taught.

So. Imagine, if you will, being 7,8 and 9 years old and ALREADY knowing that the Church that held the "God of my Fathers" was PURPOSELY leaving things out. Add to that being told, "that's just the way it is" when you ask "why" this is this way or that is that way. Even a child knows that these are not proper answers. So I went searching... Not exactly then however, when I started to realize that I WAS different than the rest of my family, I began to look. This began at the age of 11. Things happened that just was not answered by the Church or anyone affiliated with it.

Don't get me wrong. I KNEW God was real. I felt God's presence in my life, even if I felt more than a bit disconnected from the family around me. Something unusual was going on in my life. All the things I was told that was wrong to be were EXACTLY what were becoming of me. My interest didn't run to sports, cars or any of the "normal" things little boys were supposed to run to. I was more interested in boys, magick and spirituality. The kicker to this was the magick part. I KNEW there was Divine Magicks in the world. I KNEW that God inspired these magicks to aid us in our daily lives. I couldn't, for the life of me, fathom why so many people were against it. After all, they were performing magick EVERY Sunday in our local Church. The exoteric and the esoteric are what drove me towards my search. Looking for the "hidden in plain sight" as well as the "hidden from view". I could not fathom why others didn't see this magick that was right in front of their eyes.

Flash forward 10 years and I decided to go into the ministry, still knowing there were things hidden from me, having faith that I would find them. Seminary completely destroyed my faith. The things I learned during Seminary, such as the de-feminization of God and which books of the Bible actually fit the rhetoric that we were supposed to teach people. In my search for the truth, I found more lies... More misdirection. More secrets...

My faith was devastated.

I walked away from it all. In my search for the truth, I went to Wicca, Celtic Shamanism, Druidry, returned to both sides of my own heritage. Nothing quite fit my concept of God, the Divine Magicks I believed in nor the culpability that EACH person has to be a "good person". I NEEDED to find God as I understood him to be.

I NEEDED TO.

When I walked away from the typically preached about Christian version of God, I literally went on a stroll in my own hometown. I was walking for hours and had reached the outskirts of my hometown where farms had begun to pop up. One in particular grew corn... After all, Indiana Beach's advertisement for a few years was, "There's more than corn in Indiana" to which I would add... "Not much"... I remember walking through the corn, finding the most peace I had felt in a few days and a sudden… "Oneness" for lack of a better word.

I walked into this little clearing in the center of the corn field and there stood the most beautiful woman I had ever seen in my life. Dressed all in white, dreadlocked hair, coffee colored skin, almond shaped eyes of the most beautiful and deep shade of green I had ever seen… Believe it or not, I could "feel" her before I even laid eyes on her. Curious, I simply sat down and watched.

After a while, my curiosity got the better of me and I began to ask what she was doing. She told me flat out, "I'm work in a protection trick" so I watched. I took in all I could. Asked questions when she was quiet. "There are some things I will speak on others are not for me to tell you" was the response to some of my queries… This sparked within me. It rang with a truth I hadn't heard in a LONG time. Someone telling me that they could only take me so far meant that my journey MUST begin in one place and end in another.

When I moved to New Orleans, the craziest thing began to happen. A certain sequence seemed to run course through EVERY dream I had. I've discussed the dream sequence before, so I won't bring it up further here. Suffice to say, during one of the dream sequences, the Spirit waltzing through my dreams turned out to be Baron Samedi and he said to me, "You're mine." From that point on, it has been a steadily increasing part of my life. This journey with Spirit, both the Orisha and Loa, has restored my faith, built me back up to a person that I am proud to be and moved me forward in my dreams. All in all, I consider it a "win win" scenario...

Throughout my tenure in Voodoo (New Orleans own style) and the Haitian Vodou I am being taught by Mama Lola and Mambo Maggie, I have learned that it is far easier to simply serve Spirit than to serve myself. To that end, I do what I do because it is what I feel led to do.

I hope that you enjoyed a look at some of the questions I've been asked over time and the answers that go with those questions. I also hope that you learned a bit more about the path that I follow.

Again. I caution you that these answers are from my own perspective and you should endeavor to find your own answers.

"In Voodoo there is a fix for everything," Houngan Jesse

New Orleans Voodoo, as with many of the traditions, has adapted a number of devices to more appropriately fit into its teachings and workings. Due to the fluidity of New Orleans Voodoo, you find tools that most of the ATRs don't use. This is because Voodoo became open to ANYONE who felt defenseless, enslaved, underappreciated or even "less than" the people around them. It didn't matter if they were truly slaves, indentured servants or someone just lost to the world. For this reason, you find tools in New Orleans Voodoo, and in many of the offshoots, that were not originally found within the ATRs.

New Orleans Voodoo is a rich tradition filled with many intriguing tools. I briefly spoke about the incorporation of and the uses of the Voodoo doll. Now, I will speak about the Gris Gris bag. Gris Gris bags are a fundamental and iconic item in the world of New Orleans Voodoo. They are, in essence, charm bags filled with herbs and roots, anointed with oils and sealed with prayer work to effect the changes necessary in someone's life. They can be made for generally any purpose or for any person.

Gris Gris bags are also known as, Mojo bags and "Mojo Hands". I was taught a bit differently about what they actually were, so I will place that here for you to understand WHY I differentiate between a Gris Gris bag and a Mojo bag.

The way I was taught: There is a difference between Mojo bags and Gris Gris bags. A Mojo bag is created by the practitioner FOR the practitioner's own usage. It is filled with things that the practitioner feels more adequately represents their need at the time and can be changed at will, should the need arise. The Gris Gris bag is a charm bag that is made BY a practitioner FOR another person. The reason they are called the French word for "gray" is because they stand between YOUR light and the darkness around you. Each house and, indeed, even some practitioners have different recipes and names for similar acting oils, Gris Gris and dolls. So don't be surprised when someone says, "well, we call it this!"

Four such devices and their purposes are:

Love's Desire: This particular Gris Gris is created to help inspire love and passion in a relationship. Whether your relationship is just beginning or it has been on the run for a long time, this Gris Gris bag is designed to keep the roads of communication open in the relationship so that the love and passion can flourish and grow.

Love's Desire Gris Gris

Road Opener: This Gris Gris is designed to carry on the spirit of Exu's blessing and bring it into a more applicable status. "Road Opener" is the term used for a series of devices designed to help move you forward by causing things to fall into place with your wishes. Bringing your desires to fruition...

Road Opener Gris Gris

Money: This Gris Gris is truly meant to bring money into your life. Whether that is by bringing you a newer and better job, quick money from a scratch ticket or even the beginnings of your own business ventures, the Money Gris Gris is the one for you...

Money Gris Gris

Good Luck: As the name implies, this Gris Gris is blessed to bring its bearer an amount of luck that will help them prosper with the blessings of the "wee ones", as my Great Grandfather used to call them. Spirits who can, given the proper incentive, cause your probabilities to move in a more positive manner. If you're looking to pick up a few scratch off tickets, play a game of cards or drop some coins in a slot machine, the prayer work involved will help you with these issues and more.

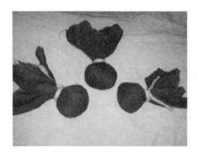

Good Luck Gris Gris

There are, of course, corresponding oils, soaps, candles for each of the Gris Gris created by any given practitioner. As working recipes are found, they may be shared throughout a practicing house or, as some people have done, shared in books or over internet websites.

The recipes I used for the 4 above mentioned Gris Gris come from my first Godmother in Voodoo, a woman whose family has been Voodoo practitioners for as long as anyone could remember. They are part of my personal repertoire of Voodoo "tricks" and will only be passed to those that become part of MY practicing house...

Other tools of the trade:

Voodoo Doll: The most notable, notorious and most misrepresented tool of the New Orleans Voodoo practitioner, and also the most misunderstood, is the Voodoo Doll. The Voodoo Doll isn't even a Voodoo "invention"; it is one of the many things that were incorporated from other people who came into the practice. It is our incorporation of the European Poppet which was brought over with indentured servants who became acquainted with the practices of the African slaves.

However...

They were not used for what they are used for in today's society. Voodoo Dolls were originally incorporated in as a means of record keeping. To help you further understand what I am speaking of, I will share with you the hypothetical situation that I share with people at Voodoo Authentica on a regular basis.

There was also no set standard on how a Voodoo Doll was made. What mattered was your proximity to the "city's center". If you lived within the city or close enough to make it a nice day out, you might make an all cloth doll because cloth would be easier to obtain. If you were further away, in the "bayou country" where cloth was treated as more of a commodity, you might make a stick and moss doll covered with a bit of cloth to represent the person or desire you were working to achieve...

An example of how the Voodoo Doll was first utilized in New Orleans Voodoo:

Let's imagine that you were out riding your horse to perform some sort of task. While riding, you fell off and injured your shoulder. You would be brought to someone such as myself, whether a priest, priestess or root-worker of any kind, and we would use herbs, oils, roots and prayer work to affect a healing. We would take a piece of the outfit that you were wearing and create a doll with it, placing a pin in the shoulder of the doll to signify where we had concentrated our healing efforts.

The next time that you came back to see us, we take the doll that represented you down from a shelf, look at where the pin placement was and ask something like, "OK, we worked on your shoulder last time, is this what we are working on again? Or are we moving on to something else?"

The more severe the injuries, the more pins you would find in the doll.

After a time, we learned what the Europeans had been doing all along with the dolls in the form of sympathetic magicks, and acknowledged that they could be used as a focal tool FOR a person. So, if the injuries were severe enough, what would happen is that the people who brought your case to our attention would bring bits of the clothing you were wearing, hair and nail clippings to us. These items would be incorporated into the doll which would then serve as a direct conduit to the injured person. Again, we would place pins in the doll to represent everywhere we were attempting to direct the healing energy.

Thus the Voodoo Doll came into standard practice in New Orleans style of Voodoo.

Contrary to popular belief, there was really no set standard on how a Voodoo Doll was made. It all depended on how close to the city center you were as to what type of doll you would make. If you were close to the city, where cloth was a easily obtained, you might make an all cloth or rag style doll. If you were out in the boonies and bayous where cloth was treated as more of a commodity, then you might vie for a stick and moss doll with a shell covering of cloth or a "cloth dress" to represent the client you were working on… It really depended on what you had on hand and how easily you could come by other things.

Potion Oils: One of the most versatile tool in the arsenal of any Voodoo practitioner, whether priest, priestess or merely a practitioner is oils. A single oil can be used to anoint candles, written decrees, altar pieces, participants in a ceremony (especially "fetes"), inserted into baths, gris gris or pretty much anything else you can name. Mixed oils are such that they can be made to a purpose, such as love oil, money oil, and fertility oil and beyond.

Powders/Dusts: Powders are another tool found in the arsenal of the Voodoo practitioner. They can be used for a number of reasons and in almost as many ways as the Oils can be. Obviously you won't be "anointing" items. Powders are sprinkled over areas and dusted over your own body and others to achieve the desires that the powders were created for. The most common powder found in the arsenal of a New Orleans practitioner is "Goofer Dust". My Godmother would state that "Goofer Dust is a powerful reflective magic. It will rebound ill intent of every sort to the sender IF it is made with respect to your Ancestors." Part of this is because one of the primary ingredients in "Goofer Dust" is graveyard dirt, so this MUST be gathered with reverence to YOUR and, indeed, ALL Ancestors in mind. Including those that you may have forgotten about…

Baths: Baths within the ATRs can be an immensely beneficial tool. They have been used for everything from aiding in matters of the heart to matters of health issues to court cases and to cleanse away unwanted negative energy/influence from your life. Whether it is a "dry bath" or a "wet bath" it is designed to be used by a single person to accomplish a specified goal. Some baths are designed to work quickly and others are meant to be done over a matter of days. Whichever bath you choose to do, follow the instructions and do them for as long as necessary for the magicks to set in.

The general rule of thumb for a bath is this: A "bad bath" (something to remove a specific negative energy in your life) is done from the top of your head to the bottoms of your feet while a "good bath" (something to boost/replace positive energy in your life) is done from the bottoms of your feet to the top of your head. Baths are generally made by practitioners in their own homes for their personal use however can be premade or made fresh in any *botanica* (store that specializes in Voodoo/Vodou or other ATRO services, items and equipment) by the practitioners working there.

Florida Water: Florida Water is a staple in New Orleans Voodoo, and in many of the offshoots of the ATRs. It has numerous uses within the system. The most common use is as a "cleansing" device. In this alone, there are several ways to use this.

It can be added to mop water and used to remove negativity during basic cleansing of the home's floors. Added to your bath water, it can be used to cleanse any negative energy from your body. Left in

57

a bowl under your bed, it aids in keeping negative energy out of your sleep time (It is suggested by THIS pet owner that if you do this, use a covered bowl, such as a food saving bowl with a lid). Splashed around a room/house/business it can keep the energy excited to the point that negativity cannot take root.

The story I heard about Florida Water: One time during a ceremony, when Spirit was at a low, the drummers and dancers were doing their best to entice Spirit to make an appearance. Try as they might, Spirit was sluggish and nigh unto non-responsive. Fevered cries to Ellegua/Papa Legba were made and yet none were answered.

A dancer, giving her all, stumbled and fell into a shelf and a bottle of Florida Water fell to the floor and shattered, spraying the aromatic tincture across the surface of Legba's Veve. In an instant, things changed. The very air crackled with new energy and Legba found his horse. The ceremony changed from that point on as new energy was infused and Legba made his appearance bringing with him a host of other Spirits to see to the needs of the practitioners and their families.

Colognes/Waters: In addition to Florida Water, there are a number of other cologne/waters that are used by practitioners of New Orleans style of Voodoo. These colognes are used to empower certain types of workings, appease specific Spirits and more. Among the various colognes/waters are Kananga Water, Rose Water and Orange Blossom Water. For over a decade and a half, they have been a staple in my own workings and will continue to be that way for as long as I travel this path.

Cascarilla: Another tool found in the arsenal of the Voodoo practitioner and again, throughout the other offshoots of the ATRs, is Cascarilla. Cascarilla is a chalky substance generally made from powdered egg shells and, much like Florida Water, has multiple uses.

Crushed into the bath water along with Florida Water, it can be used to cleanse you from negative energy, including negative spirits which may have attached themselves to you for whatever reason. Used to mark crosses on the entrances/exits of your home, it can protect your home from negative energy, either sent or accidentally stumbled into. Marking crosses on your or someone else' forehead, hands and soles of the feet prevent psychic attacks. Marking crosses on the walls and then placing mirrors on them prevent people from scrying into your home. Pretty much any place you can think of to make a mark can be marked with a cross to prevent negative energy and intent.

Sage. Although commonly thought to be a cleansing agent (and, indeed, it CAN be used to cleanse an area when used with OTHER cleansers) it is used more often to purify an area. After cleansing an area with Cascarilla and Florida Water, or whatever you have decided to use, follow it by smudging the area with sage (I prefer organic white sage due to the aroma) to purify your space and lock it down from negative activity, energy and intent.

Think about it this way, if you will allow. You walk into an area that is already filled with love, hope and healing and decide to sage the area. This will make the area more pure in those intentions... Conversely however, if you walk into an area that is filled with negative intentions, anger, anxiety and sadness and then use sage, you purify those emotions and negative intentions... Meaning. You **ACTUALLY** make them stronger.

Sea Salt. Here is another of those versatile tools found in Voodoo. My Godmother adored its use in cleansing rituals, making bath salts and cleansing baths, adding some to lit charcoal to drive restless spirits back to their places of rest and more. Once you've cleansed your home, through which ever methods you desire or using Florida Water and Cascarilla, you can toss a bit of sea salt in the corners of every room to help keep spirits out of your home.

Rum, Gin and Cigars... Staples in the Voodoo that I do, these elements are used to salute and call on spirits, bless artifacts and more. In saluting the Spirits, some rum or gin is placed in a glass, poured out on the floor and sprayed, by the mouth, on people, items needing consecration and altars during workings. The cigar can be a bit on the difficult side as the cherry is placed in the mouth and a "shotgun" is blown. This can also be done for the situations which I have listed off above.

Veve for Baron Samedi

"Great Spirit on High, God, Olodumare, grant peace, protection and prosperity to all who pass me by so that they will know your great works" Mama Anna Marie

As I have explained earlier, I grew up with an expanded consciousness of what "God" meant to me. For the life of me, I could never fit Him/Her in that meager little box that so many people seem so willing to stick Him/Her in. I could also never fully connect with the idea that our one supreme being was a little bald white man in the clouds waiting to swat us into eternal damnation for not blindly following behind people blindly leading us down a very narrow and, seemingly, steeply inclined, winding path... It just did not click with me no matter how hard I tried. I could also not reconcile placing all too human traits on a supreme being who was supposed to be "of love"... Traits like discrimination, hate and superiority. This does not mean that it is wrong in any way, shape or form or wrong for other people for that matter. It meant that it was just wrong for ME. This is where I began to lose faith in the "God of my Fathers" and began my search for answers. What I found combined with what I experienced in my life led to a complete shattering of my faith. I traversed several paths before coming to Voodoo and among them was a return to both sides of my roots. Nothing seemed to fit with my "expanded consciousness of God" and I was feeling even more discouraged than usual on the spiritual side of my life.

And then the dream sequence began. Yeah. Sequence is the right word because it wasn't a full dream and it happened in EVERY dream for a period of 4 years. It did not matter whether it was my brain blowing fluff around from the day, a psychic intent or a full-fledged nightmare, the same occurrence would happen.

You must understand. I've trained myself to initialize certain visualizations should something be important; another for nightmares and yet another for my brain blowing fluff. When this new sequence began, it took me by surprise. Not the fact that a dream sequence was happening. What surprised me was that it was happening frequently.

Somewhere along the course of a dream clouds would roll overhead and fog would begin to swirl around my feet and up to my knees and this man would traipse through. Sauntering by as if nothing was going on, occasionally glancing over depending on the dream I was in the throes of and move on as if merely enjoying a midnight stroll.

One night, during a particularly nasty bout of destroying and running terrified from zombies and other creatures deemed "hellish" by those of conventional definitions in my dreams, the event began only this time... This time there was one major difference. The person stepping through my dreams stopped, looked square at me and stated, quite simply and with absolute surety, "You are mine."

Things, from that moment on, changed for me in ways that I can only describe as "God sent". Everything, and I do mean EVERYTHING, became clear as though reading through the finest glass.

The next day, I went out to meet with a VERY eclectic group of practicing pagans. We had a regular meeting night once a month at our local Denny's... Of course this meeting took place at 4 AM!!! So. Over a cup of coffee and a Grand Slam, the subject of dreams came up. Around the table fantastic dreams of fancy took flight as one after another of the pagans began to discuss their dreams.

And then MY turn came. All I could think of to say was, "I haven't had anything fantastical in the form of dreams taking place however, I have had a strange occurrence in EVERY dream lately" and I told them what had happened.

My favorite person there, Miss Eleanor, a rather large and jovial woman began what I could only describe as a TRUE witches cackle and she barked out, "Zaah, behbeh, we done told ya dat duh Baron walk round here like no bodies bidness." So I had a place to begin my search. The Baron...

But WHICH Baron? In my research, I found out that there was MORE THAN ONE. Baron Cemetrie. Baron La Croix. Baron Criminal. Baron Samedi. To name some of the more prominent ones. I began comparing any and all information that I could glean from the interwebs, which then admittedly was LITTLE TO NONE. After all, there wasn't this big push towards "bing" or "google" and most of the information to be found was simply "word of mouth"... I did find that one of the Saints that had been synchronized with the Orisha and Loa was St Expedite. Through some of the other practices I had picked up the basics on making an altar so that is EXACTLY what I set out to do. My first altar was sparse indeed. A statue of St Expedite stood in the center of a shelf decorated with black and purple cloth (because of my own personal choice before I learned that they were Ghede colors), a cup for water, a plate for food offerings and a candle. That was pretty much it. I stumbled across some information that moved me to do my prayer work with Baron Samedi, the one I seemed to identify with the most. I found that the day of Ghede working was Saturday, in fact, that is what Samedi translated out to be... Baron Saturday.

This is how my path began. A little over a year later, a woman, Mama Anna Marie, my first "Godmother" in Voodoo, came up to me in Jackson Square and stated quite firmly, "Yo Daddy done told me I gots ta teach you da right way now." I thought the woman was absolutely crazy because I hadn't spoke to my Father in YEARS... When I stated so, she simple stated, "Not dat Daddy, yo OTHER one." It clicked the instant she say that. Baron Samedi had said I was his so this must be the "daddy" she was telling me about.

I began a long and earnest study of New Orleans style of Voodoo at that point. My first Godmother would send me here and there, running errands for items from this place or that. It was an apprenticeship to see if I was truly serious about learning. Once she figured out that I WAS truly serious, she began my training, showing me the ins and outs of a system that has been my stabilizing force for more than a decade and a half.

In 2007, I was blessed to hook up with another group of practitioners who followed a similar path as what I was taught. Brandi Kelley and Dr Glover of Voodoo Authentica came "a callin"… It was for the filming of a particular television segment however, it worked into so much more. The Voodoo Authentica family of practitioners became my surrogate family and I was even "adopted" as a Godson to Mama Lola and her daughter, Mambo Maggie.

I have continued my education in Voodoo and am now pursuing my initiations in the Haitian traditions. I will follow wherever Spirit leads me…

The Music of Voodoo

"Let the beat hit 'em
Let the music take control
The beat goes round and round
And up and down and let the beat hit em
Got to learn to let go" Lisa Lisa and the Cult Jam

In every Voodoo ceremony, from the minor "get together" to the major celebrations, called "fetes", you will find that music plays a rather large part in Voodoo and many of the offshoots of the ATRs. From simple songs to the Orisha and Loa to the lavish beatings of drums to combinations of the two including dancers, the music of Voodoo is a contagious means of transporting one from the mundane mindset to the otherworldly thought processes capable of creating the changes desired during a ceremony.

Even in my own home and practice, the drums are saluted, used and celebrated as a way of communing with those Spiritual Forces called the Orisha and the Loa.

Veve for the drums

Songs for each of the Orisha and Loa are taught to practitioners by their leaders, Priests, Priestesses, Houngans, Mambos, Godmothers and Godfathers. Each practicing house may use subtle variations of songs for each of the Spirits or they may be exact duplicates of time honored songs passed down from family member to family member from the original Diasporic peoples. The unfortunate thing about the English language is that many practitioners from English speaking countries attempt to put their particular speech patterns in play in songs created from different language origins. A wonderful collection of songs for the Orisha can be found in the book "Orin Orisa: Songs for Selected Heads" (John Mason). In the book, Mason even strives to teach a person how to properly pronounce words which were traditional African.

With the fluidity of the English language however, there came a slide that many of the American practitioners just can't seem to get away from. This comes from several factors. The first and foremost was that ANY African slave caught speaking in his or her native tongue was tortured brutally. This caused much of the American information for practitioners to be fractured. Words once pronounced forcefully and effectively became slurred, mixed with the understanding of the overseers and owners of slaves… Take for example… Anansi. Anansi is a wisdom teaching Spirit. When the African slaves were speaking of the "Wisdoms of Anansi" pronounced ah-NON-seh, the English speaking slave owners thought they were saying "Aunt Nancy"… So, a subtle shift later and the slaves hid Anansi behind Aunt Nancy…

Song lyrics like "ovwi baryea pou Atibon" one of the songs for Papa Legba shifted to "o way bayeh por Atibon"… All a matter of displacement, banning of traditions/speech/habits/religions and enforced servitude… Because of this, knowledge was lost, shifted and continued in as fluid a way as possible.

During a ceremony where you find drummers, dancers, vocalists, salutes are given to each of these to honor the spirit of the ceremony and the Spirits that will guide the ceremony to its fruition. This can be done simply or in a more ritualistic fashion. It can be as simple as pouring a libation at each of the drums, giving the drummers a taste of the libation and knocking three times at each drum although I have seen some truly complicated rituals honoring the battery of drums and drummers…

The drummers are a blessed addition to ANY ceremony or fete and will, in turn, bring one closer to Spirit, if you allow them. Drums, and indeed music, are such a part of any ceremony that even statues of the Orisha Chango/Shango can be found with him and several drummers.

Songs are sung for EACH sprit called during a ceremony ALWAYS beginning with the Guardian of the Gateways.

An Introduction to Spirit

It is important to understand that even though there are certain aspects of Voodoo that will ALWAYS be taught the same way, identification of the Spirit Forces has never been "set in stone", so to speak. Even within like families, the Spirit Forces (the Orisha and Loa) are spoken of in different manners and different tones. One example of this can be found in the Spirit Force, Oshun. In some of the teachings of Oshun, she is seen as an example of women's mysteries while in other teachings she is seen as a "slut"...

I am not going to do anything other than talk about how *I*, personally, identify with the Orisha and the Loa. This journey through Voodoo, to me, has made one thing PERFECTLY clear. Whenever the Orisha and Loa come into your life, they take on a part of you and YOU begin to take on a part of them as well...

As New Orleans style of Voodoo is a combination of the African and Haitian Traditions, I will endeavor to speak on them from my personal understanding of them and how I identify with them, as well as show you which ones are "sort of" cross-over Spirits. I will begin working with the 7 African Powers as identified by my Godmother, Mama Anna Marie Johnson, Louisah Teish (who wrote

"Jambalaya") and Voodoo Authentica (www.voodooshop.com), working in the "cross-over" Spirits and then finally into the more Haitian element. The Loa not already discussed with the 7 African Powers previously discussed.

I should also state here that, as with many other things, the understanding of the Orisha and the Loa has shifted over the course of the centuries. The more we learn, the more they shift adapting to the new knowledge. This is just another reason that I call any of the ATRS and their offshoots as LIVING religions. Living belief system.

** I would like to add here that ANY and ALL Veve that I have listed here in this book can be found online with a simple search and the use of them in this book falls under "fair use" for this very reason. Veve are "sigils" representing a connection to specific Spiritual forces found within Voodoo and many of the offshoots of the ATRs... The Original Traditions used other forms of symbolism to denote the Orisha**

The African side with a twist

Here, I will discuss the Orisha, which was the base for New Orleans style of Voodoo. I will also add the names of the Loa which are aligned with some of the Orisha. It is imperative to note, yet again, that while these Spirits are often seen on the same altars in New Orleans practitioner's homes, we recognize that they ARE their own unique entity and have their own modes of service, favorite foods, and libations and hold their own attitudes and representative requirements.

Ellegua/Papa Legba

Whenever you are looking for answers or a difficult decision needs to be made and you want that wisdom/sense of your grandfather, Ellegua and Papa Legba is who you turn to. They are in charge of communication, especially between this realm and the spirit realm where the Orisha and Loa abide… Make no mistake, though similar in nature, Ellegua, Papa Legba and Eshu may work with the same energy of the Crossroads however; they are not the same Spirit. They ARE different enough to hold their own individual station in the pantheon of Spirits called the Orisha and Loa. As are many other spirits with similar functions yet differing names.

Ellegua/Papa Legba is often pictured as an older man with a bad leg, using a cane to mobilize… During rituals, when he finds his horse, it is not uncommon for Ellegua/Papa Legba to ask for a chair or stool to sit on while he does his work, speaks with the people or even creates objects that will help people with what they need…

Ellegua/Papa Legba is a "Gateway Spirit" and considered the "Door Opener". Sought when things seem to be closing down all around you, he is that Spirit who will either tell you WHY or tell you how to open doors to clear the path for you. As a "Gateway Spirit", he is that Spirit that guards the "Crossroads" of your life. This being the case, he is ALWAYS saluted first during ceremonies. It is said, and per my own experiences AFTER being properly trained/taught, if Ellegua/Papa Legba is not entreated first, no other Spirit will make an appearance.

Lately, since the earthquake that has ravaged Haiti, Papa Legba has made a subtle shift to remind us that the Orisha/Loa understands our plights. Papa Legba has become a SERIOUS force to be reckoned with in the rebuilding of Haiti… Up to and including stamping around on two good legs and appearing younger in actions and attitudes. Even in dreams, Papa Legba's appearance has become younger, more able bodied showing his support for the plight of our Haitian brothers and sisters and reminding us that Spirit is ALWAYS aware… Even today…

As an interesting aside, and more to prove the point that we take on aspects of the Orisha/Loa, many of my friends and readers of this

76

book will know that I, by choice, am a reader in Jackson Square. Once I came to the understanding that *I* was the crossroad of communication for these people who seek answers in their life, I suddenly became VERY aware that I, in fact, took on an aspect of Ellegua/Papa Legba. Since then, I have been totally comfortable with reading for people AND have not been afraid to speak the messages that I am receiving... This, more than anything else, has helped me develop my own style of reading and how to tell people news that they may not want to hear...

Veve for Papa Legba

Ellegua/Papa Legba Common Knowledge:

Day of the Week: Monday

Place of Power: Any Crossroad

Place in the Home: Behind the front door

Colors: Red and Black

Number: 3

Saint: St Michael, St Peter, San Martine

Ogun/Papa Ogou:

Ogun/Papa Ogou is a warrior spirit like no other. He is the General marshalling his troops for battle. Whatever conflict you are going through, Ogun/Papa Ogou is the one you need at your side (and sometimes standing directly in front of you). He is a devout protector, especially of police, military, fire fighters, EMTs and any First Responders. Ogun/Papa Ogou WILL protect you. This is truly anon negotiable fact of his energies.

One of the more entertaining aspects of Ogun/Papa Ogou is that he is considered the "Father of Technology". For this reason, I tend to keep something of him near my computer to aid in its continued operation. Otherwise, for some uncanny reason, I burn through them far too quickly. As the "Father of Technology", Ogun/Papa Ogou was said to have taught us how to build homes, farms, the tools necessary to BUILD those homes and farms.

Depending on which tradition you follow, the Warrior Spirits are Ogun/Papa Ogou, Ochosi and Chango/Shango or Ogun/Papa Ogou, Ellegua and Chango/Shango. Make no mistake however, as I've mentioned earlier, there are literally hundreds, if not thousands, of Orisha and Loa... There ARE more Warrior Spirits among them. If one makes themselves known to you, by all means, see what aid he or she may offer.

Ogun/Papa Ogou is the master of metal and the ultimate blacksmith working the metals into precious designs, vaunted tools and deadly weapons. This is one of the primary reasons that Ogun/Papa Ogou is considered the "Father of Technology"...

Ogun/Papa Ogou, being a Warrior Spirit will often have a machete on his altar as it is his weapon of choice.

Veve for Ogou Ferray

Ogun/Papa Ogou Common Knowledge:

Day of the Week: Tuesday (Haitian day is Wednesday)

Place of Power: United States, Deep Woods

Place in the Home: Behind the front door, workshops, offices near technology

Colors: Green and Black

Number: 3 or 4

Saint: St Anthony, St George

Yemaya:

Yemaya is always and forever the Eternal Mother, as deep as any ocean and bountiful as any sea. Her love knows no boundaries. Yet, like the oceans and the seas, Yemaya can be a stormy task master.

Often sought in matters of fertility because she has shown an affinity for would-be mothers, Yemaya shows her everlasting strength, abundant love and fierce loyalty to those who she calls. Fiercely protective would be the ultimate way to describe how Yemaya watches over mothers and those seeking the blessing of a child.

She is an even fiercer protector of the children IN the home after they are born… Much like the lioness protects her cubs, Yemaya is equally fierce and watchful when it comes to the Children of a home. Many practitioners will place effigies of Yemaya or pictures of her correlating Saint on a high shelf in the child or children's bedroom so that she can keep a wary eye on them.

Because of her motherly nature, concerns of the home become the domain of the Orisha Yemaya. Concerns such as protection of the home, peace within the home, prosperity of the home all fall under her   domain.

Being that Yemaya is an African Orisha, she really doesn't have a "veve"… There are some out there depending on traditions. More often than not, in New Orleans traditions, Yemaya is represented by a mermaid. Many of the Orisha, you will find, have no "veve" being that this is more a Haitian traditional aspect. It would also be good to note here that there ARE other systems that are offshoots of the ATRs that have their own personal sigils when it comes to the Orisha, Loa or their particular name for the Spirits. Palo is a very good example of this.

Yemaya Common Knowledge:

Day of the Week: Saturday

Place of power: Brazil, Oceans and Seas

Place in the Home: Bedroom, Children's Room, Bathroom, Kitchen

Colors: Blue and White

Number: 7

Saint: Lady of Regla, Mary Star of the Sea

As a side note… Many of the homes I have partaken in, including my own, have revolved around the kitchen and as that is the case, Yemaya's presence has ALWAYS been felt here. This is why it is added as a "Place in the Home" for her.

Chango/Shango:

Chango/Shango is a mighty warrior and the Spirit of Justice within the New Orleans pantheon of Orisha and Loa. He is fiery male passion, and linked to the elements of fire, thunder and lightning.

Chango/Shango is often called upon during issues of a legal nature and worked with to "heat up" other workings due to his fiery nature. He is often sought out when a man's "fires" have cooled to bring his passion back to life. Chango/Shango helps with the virility of man as well…

Reputed to be a living person at one time, Chango/Shango was said to be a great king (Alafin) in Africa whose rule was just and he was well loved by his people. He was also said to have a fiery temper. The story goes that one day, Chango/Shango was blinded by his rage to the point that he accidentally killed his best friend. In sorrow he sought a way to right this great wrong. The only thought he could come up with was to dissolve all his holdings, give it to the family of his best friends, walked into the woods and hung himself.

Chango's/Shango's people were so distraught by this action that they began to lament his passing. While in the middle of their lamentations, Ogun appeared out of the woods and stated, "Rejoice! Your king is among us now." In that moment Chango's/Shango's body disappeared in a burst of lightning and fire and he was reborn as a Spirit of Justice. Lightning is thought to be the living representation of "divine justice".

This is but one rendition of this particular tale. Some of the renditions state that it was a brother that he accidentally killed. Others say it is because he forced his two brothers to fight to the death. Understanding the fluidity, with which the tales were spread and changed throughout time, especially here in the United States, allows the seeker to find each of the tales containing the same basic structure and lesson to it and, it is my hope, that you enjoy the reading OF each of these tales.

In yet other stories, Chango/Shango is seen as almost a transitory path from the innocence and naiveté of a child to the blossoming into man-/womanhood a widely circulated story showing this remarkable change would be the story of the "Mad Man of Ijebu" a traditional *Ifa* tale of Chango/Shango.

Chango/Shango, like each of the Warrior Spirits will usually have a representation of a weapon on his altar. His particular weapon of choice is the double headed axe.

Chango/Shango common knowledge:

Day of the Week: Friday

Place of Power: Trinidad, sky and trees

Place in the Home: Fireplace, business desk

Colors: Red and White

Number: 6

Saint: Santa Barbara, St Jerome

Oya

Oya, one of my absolute favorite Spirits to deal with here in New Orleans, is the African Orisha who is most notably a Queen. Oya is called the "Queen of the Market Place" demarking THREE major ideologies.

Women were the major authorities in business. Conducting business on behalf of the family while the hunter/warriors were off gathering meat/provisions or battling some opposing force.

Women were WHOLLY integrated and incorporated as equals in life. Sharing power with their husbands in many ways.

As "Queen of the Market Place," Oya was good to be in ANY business. ESPECIALLY if that business was owned/operated by women.

Oya was also said to be the "Queen of the Winds and Hurricanes" and as such, represented change and transition, sometimes, in a complete upheaval of our lives. Sometimes she saw fit to change things subtly, as if by a gentle breeze. While at other times, it is as if she needs to send a Category 5 Hurricane into our lives to blow everything away that has held us back for so long.

The "crowning glory' to Oya, to me, is in her title as "Queen of the Cemeteries". It is in this role that Oya stands out amongst the other Orisha. Being the "Queen of the Cemeteries", Oya is the ultimate "go to" person for connecting with our Ancestors and dearly departed. Whenever we beseech her in the name of our Ancestors, action ALWAYS happens amongst the dead. She brings their energies into sharp focus on whatever we have sought for them to work on. Be it situations of love, prosperity, protection, healing or you name it…

There is an old saying in Voodoo, "nothing brought to the Ancestors will sit for long". I think that this is because Voodoo (as many of the offshoots of the ATRs) believes that death merely ends the physicality of something, not the spirituality nor the other energetic parts of a person's identity. Therefore, after death there is still a way for the departed to make things right with us. Indeed, in many cases, when we go to the dead, it is often those who wronged us in life that will make the headlong plunge into whatever we are attempting to do. In other words, even after death there is a way to atone for any past wrongs to get right with Olodumare/God/the Creative Source (whatever name you wish to put on that all encompassing spirit that created and works through everything).

Many people don't understand how we can believe that however, it is based on a Biblical statement 1 Thessalonians 4:16 *"For the Lord Himself will descend from heaven with a shout, with the voice of the archangel and with the trumpet of God, and the dead in Christ will rise first."* If 'the dead in Christ will rise first', where are they now? According to Voodoo beliefs, they are still here in Spirit, watching over us... They are simply waiting for us to reconnect with their energies and ASK FOR HELP in matters that we, simply, cannot attain on our own energies or our own connection with the Divine.

Oya common knowledge:

Day of the Week: Wednesday

Place of Power: River Niger, the Amazon, anywhere the wind is blowing

Place in the Home: Library, Study

Colors: Red, purple, brown, deep ambers and burnt orange

Number: 9

Saint: St Theresa, St Catherine, Lady of Candelaria

Obatala:

Obatala, in New Orleans Voodoo, is a Spirit of cleansing, healing, balance, perception, ancient wisdom and deep knowledge. One will often hear, "Obatala rules all heads", this is a nod back to the fact that Obatala is the Ifa representation of the "spark of life" that travels through each and every living thing on the face of the planet. His white robes are symbols of the creative energy used throughout the creation process and an echo to that "spark of life" in each of us. Sought out in matters of wisdom, knowledge, balance and healing, Obatala encapsulates that drive that spurs a person to new heights, always learning and achieving wisdom along the way. Between Ochosi and Obatala, all ailments are covered.

It would be good to remind people that, because Obatala is also about Spiritual Balance, Renewal and Spiritual Cleansing, Obatala is often called on to help divest a person of the Spiritual effects of an ailment. That depression, lethargy, "why me, Lord?" and other like thoughts and patterns that can accompany an illness. Especially a long term or chronic illness.

When worry over an issue becomes a predominant factor to or in that issue, it is always good to seek out Obatala's wisdom and council to alleviate the unnecessary worry. If an ailment comes saddled with depression, anger, frustration or anything of this nature, it is prudent to seek Obatala to help reclaim a balance to the person's being. When energy around you just seems to stagnate and you've tried everything you know to cause movement again, you may wish to seek Obatala out to renew the energy of the space. These are just a few examples on why someone would go to Obatala of the White Robes and they are, by far, not a complete listing of reasons…

It seems, through many of the stories, that Obatala was a drunken and rambunctious Spirit when originally tasked with the creation process by Olodumare, which in turn caused Olodumare to abandon the idea of Obatala finishing the creation process and thus turning to Oduduwa… When he sobered up and saw the things he had done, Obatala made a solemn vow to NEVER drink again thus setting aside his rambunctious nature and becoming the Spirit of Balance that many seek him out for.

Obatala common knowledge:

Day of the Week: Sunday

Place of Power: Clouds, Ile-Ife, Nigeria

Place in the Home: Living room, Family room, Library

Color: White with silver or purple

Number: 8

Saint: Our Lady of Mercy

Conversely... As Obatala is about Ancient Wisdom and Deep Knowledge, I have him equally represented in my home library of spiritual books. He and Damballa Wedo have found loving respect in my library and, in turn, have helped me find EXACTLY what I was looking for when I was looking for it through the myriad of books I have on a vast array of subjects from alchemy to herbalism to healing to astral projection to you name it...

Oshun:

Oshun is the African Orisha of love, sensuality, beauty, romance and prosperity in a singular sense. She is linked to the natural world through rivers, creeks and streams. Oshun, depending on the culture you are from and the teaching therein, represents the mysteries of womanhood - that whole sensual vibe that can lead to, and often does, that sexual power that many women naturally give off. From the subtle walk to the more pronounced "prowl"; from the shimmy of the hip to the sway of the breast, Oshun embodies and emboldens women to accept and flaunt their assets. She is the power of woman.

Oshun is also considered by many a patron of the arts, often equated with the Muses of Greek Mythology. Her flow is said to be so strong that it can take the artisan to the depths of their craft and STILL they would not know the end of it. To me, this gives nod to the fact that the rivers flow into the oceans and seas, the domain of Yemaya who is the keeper of the depths…

Rituals to Oshun include tossing things in a nearby river to facilitate the drawing away of negative energies, speed healing, and draw in prosperity, and drive away an enemy/negative person and to draw love to a person.

Throughout many of the African teachings, Oshun is not only seen as a sensual being, she is also seen as a warrior. Indeed, it is believed that EACH of the Orisha has some sort of warrior aspect within them. One of my favorite stories of Oshun shows just how dedicated she can be as a warrior.

The Village of Women and all of the Orisha prepared for battle. It was a battle that the Hosts of Heaven knew that they could not win. The male warriors lined up and charged repeatedly in an attempt to overpower the women. To no avail. The female warriors lined up and charged repeatedly in an attempt to overpower the women. Again, to no avail. Oshun, seeing the Hosts of Heaven defeated by the Village of Women stood up and proudly stated, "I will put a stop to this in my own way." She began by gathering water in a calabash shell. Balancing this shell full of water on her head, she began to tap a rhythm out on it. Matching the rhythm she took step after step, beginning to dance and swirl, flow and whirl, as the rivers do. Her voice lifted in song. She flowed this way from the Heavens to the Earth and began to fill the Heavens with her voice lifted in song. As she got to the gates of the Village of Women, the most miraculous thing happened. The women lay down their weapons and began to dance and sing WITH Oshun. She led them through the city, dancing and singing all the way to the Temple of Oshun. Oshun won the day without so much as lifting a blade or weapon of any kind. She won by the sheer power of her womanhood. To this day, it is said that the Village of Women STILL dance and sing at the Temple of Oshun.

** It is my personal opinion, that this story and many others like it show the powers of woman during her menstrual cycle. The greatest single criminal act of Western Traditions was to disenfranchise the power of "woman" by perverting the power of her flow. In pushing the "dirty blood" side of things, Western Traditions greatly undermined teachings that empowered women enabling them to handle EVERYTHING life could throw at them which, in turn, falsely promoted this whole concept of "weaker sex"**

Oshun common knowledge:

Day of the Week: Thursday

Place of Power: Cuba, Oshun River, Oshogbo, Nigeria, any river city, such as New Orleans

Place in the Home: Kitchen, Bedroom

Color: Yellow, green, coral, orange, gold

Number: 5

Saint: Lady of Cardidad del Cobre, Mother of Charity

Ochosi:

Ochosi is the Spirit of the Hunt in Voodoo and is one of the primary Warrior Spirits in the New Orleans style of Voodoo that I was taught. His favored weapon was the bow and his arrows were said to NEVER miss their mark. Many people go to Ochosi when they are looking for a direction in life as it is also said that "Ochosi's arrows always find the most direct route out of any situation..." Be warned however, just because the find the most direct route out does not make it the easiest route out of any situation...

As Ochosi is the Spirit of the Hunt, he is a protector of not only the animals in the wild but the hunters as well. He will teach a hunter how to properly track and take down his prey so as not to cause undue stress or suffering. Ochosi will show you the best prey and hunting   trails.

Ochosi is an avid healer, as well. His typical treatment of any injury, illness or even negative energy is through herbalism. Ochosi's knowledge of the herbs, roots and animal essences are so vast that he is considered a "magician/sorcerer". Such is his skill that he could combine any herbs, roots and ingredients to make any remedy needed. His healing prowess was so sought after that many people would just walk into the woods in an effort to learn even a portion of   Ochosi's   knowledge.

Ochosi, because his arrows are said to "never miss their mark", is also considered both a "Spirit of Justice" and a "Spirit of Revenge"… Just remember. If you seek revenge, it may come back to bite you in the ass in the end, just as in this story of Ochosi from the   Ifa   tradtions.

Ochosi had two great loves of his life. His parrot and his Grandmother. Food was running scarce in Ochosi's village so he decided to go on a hunt. Knowing that the game had moved off farther from its usual grounds, Ochosi knew that he would be gone for a long time. He went to his Grandmother and asked her to look after   his   parrot.

The game had moved so far from its normal grounds that Ochosi began to worry whether or not he would find any in time to feed his entire village yet still he pressed on. Tracking and trailing through twisting turns, Ochosi pushed on.

After an extended amount of time away from home, Ochosi found some game to hunt. With a single arrow, winged on its way with a prayer, the game was brought down. Ochosi made his way quickly home with thoughts of celebration and ceremony on his mind. When he arrived at his village, Ochosi went to his home and looked to the cage of his beloved parrot. Horror filled Ochosi's heart at the vision that awaited him. The cage of his beloved parrot was filled with feathers and blood. Horror turned to grief and then fully into rage.

A rage so deep filled Ochosi so that he put a special potion on a single arrow. He called out to Olodumare to let his aim be true to avenge his beloved pet. With a twang of the bow, Ochosi let the arrow fly and followed the path it took. He heard the strike and KNEW the arrow had struck home. When he finished his path, following his arrow, horror once again filled his heart.

There, lying in the path with an arrow in her chest was Ochosi's Grandmother.

Ochosi common knowledge:

Day of the Week: Monday, Wednesday, the 4th of every month

Place of Power: Woodland areas, forests, jungles

Place in the Home: Any high place (Ochosi likes to see the whole terrain of the place he resides and protects)

Color: Green, red, blue, violet, browns (I've even placed forest camouflage on and around his altar)

Number: 3

Saint: St Sebastian, Saint Norbert

The Haitian Side

The following listing are Loa commonly used within the New Orleans Voodoo practices stemming from the Haitian Traditions which came over at the start of the 1800s with the advent of the Haitian Revolution...

I will not be putting this in any kind of real order as I speak about them. It is important to understand that when the Haitians brought over their form of Vodou to New Orleans they brought over Spirits that opened up to a WHOLE FAMILY of "like" Spirits... A good example of this would be the Spirit Ogou. Papa Ogou can come in as, Ogou Badagris, Ogou Ferray or Ogou St Jacques to name a few. Each aspect brings in specifics that can only be found BY those specific Spirits.

Veve for Damballa

Damballa and Ayida Wedo:

Make no mistake; Damballa (also spelled Danballah, Damballa Wedo and even Dambalah) is one of the oldest Spirits to transfer from the African pantheon of Orisha into the Haitian Traditions of the Loa. Much like Obatala, Damballa is about the mind... His domains include "Ancient Wisdoms", "Deep Knowledge", balance and renewal. Some of the different tales of Damballa state that he is the father of all of the Loa and a creationist entity. More tales discuss Damballa carrying the Ancestors (those who have passed away) on his back to the other side... To Heaven, if you will.

Damballa was one of the Spirits that came over to New Orleans by way of Haiti and the Haitian Revolution. It is rumored that Marie Laveau and her family of practitioners were the first ones to truly incorporate Damballa's wisdom and healing into their works with such things as the Damballa Dance.

Damballa, especially in the Haitian Traditions and New Orleans, is often portrayed as a serpent... Indeed, the saying "the serpent and the rainbow" are nods to Damballa and his wife, Ayida Wedo. Together they represent the ultimate balance in ALL things in creation.

Damballa is a known guardian of those with physical disabilities from being crippled to deformities to handicaps of any kind... Children are also on his hit parade for protection. For this aspect and the belief that he is the father of all of the Loa, he is often called "Papa Damballa"... Like many of the Loa, the personification allows for a closer relationship to form more easily.

La Sirene

La Sirene is the embodiment of the Oceans and Seas and has an ebb and flow as strong as the lunar cycle which influences her. She reaches the depths of one's soul and helps them to come to understand themselves better. Often pictured as a mermaid, she is the ruler over the riches of the oceans and seas, deciding whom to bless and when. La Sirene is an enchantress of immense strength and is often sought after to help add power to a magickal working. As her name implies, she can sing a song so bewitching as to lure people to her for any reason she so desires.

Another of the African Spirits to cross over with the slave trade, and richly misunderstood by many practitioners today, La Sirene is often seen as haughty and vain because she is often pictured either with or viewing herself in a mirror. The mirror is said to reflect the depths with which her love, gratitude and soul delve to help another person understand themselves.

Altars for La Sirene are adorned with a myriad of ocean and sea items from shells to starfish to netting to any item used by seafarers and fishers today. Remember however, La Sirene is a BEAUTIFUL and BOLD woman. She still likes to receive the fineries that many women are attracted to. When approaching her for any endeavor, approach with respect, dignity and humility or else she WILL show you why she can be feared by taking away all of the blessing she has bestowed on you in a single instant... She, like any of the Orisha and Loa, is NOT to be trifled with.

There is one additional warning when working with La Sirene that should be broached. It is said that, SOMETIMES, those working with her become lost in the deepest desires of their heart becoming slaves to them in their own right.

Veve for Ogou Badagris

Papa Ogou

I mentioned earlier in this writing that sometimes the Loa represent a whole family of Spirit Forces. Ogou is often broke down into three particular Spirits… Ogou Ferray, Ogou Badagris and Ogou St Jacques.

Always the "General", Papa Ogou is first and foremost a protector. I was taught that each of the three aspects that I have listed off protects in specific ways and I will present them here for you to see.

Ogou Ferray is the "Sword". His protection is close to home however, he can extend enough to strike down any enemy who steps to you. Being the master of metal, Ogou's sword is of the strongest quality and will never fail to protect you from enemies as they close in on you. He moves with a quickness and surety that is as beautiful as any dance and as deadly as a viper strike.

Ogou Badagris is the "Shield". Even in his Veve, Ogou Badagris shows his propensity to protect. As with any shield, he stands before you with the force of a titanium wall blocking any and all attacks with an ease like no other aspect. Ogou Badagris, though a HIGHLY, active Spirit is just as comfortable standing right by your side not moving unless you do. Being the shield aspect of the Ogou family of Spirits, Badagris is very relaxed until such time as it is necessary to take up his shield to protect you, your loved ones or whatever you are looking to protect.

Ogou St Jacques is the "Spear". With lightning speed and quicker thinking, Ogou St Jacques strides forward to face dangers that have made themselves known which have not yet crossed into your "event horizon" at this time. Sought out for battle field knowledge, Ogou St Jacques' wisdom in battle is second to none. From his position overlooking the battle field, he can direct all of the Warrior Spirits to better fight a battle.

Together, the three elements of Papa Ogou work in tandem to provide the practitioner with the utmost protection that any element can provide. With all the strength of the iron that he represents, and then some, Papa Ogou works to protect you.

Another aspect of Papa Ogou that many people fail to realize is that he helps to forge you into the person YOU wish/desire/need to be. He is a master at shaping the raw ore which is a person into that which Olodumare has created them for.

Veve for Erzulie Freda/Ezrulie Freda Dahomey

Erzulie

Erzulie is another Loa that can be split into multiple parts. The three aspects that I have dealt with are as follows. Erzulie Freda, Erzulie Dantor and Erzulie Mapiang .

Let me explain a little deeper, if you will allow. The Erzulie Spirits stem from a Spirit much older which comes from the African Traditional Religions. The Spirit is called Ezili, linked to the Moon and all things feminine. During the time of the Haitian Revolution, the Haitians prayed to Ezili to aid them in their efforts. The first Erzulie to step forward was Freda, bringing with her the knowledge of love, prosperity, the power of the feminine to help smooth things between the Haitians and their persecutors.

Erzulie Freda told the Haitians to speak with her sister, Erzulie Dantor. Erzulie Dantor came forward with fire and vengeance at the loss of children and their mothers in the fighting that had occupied the island nation.

So. To get down to brass tax, let me explain MY understanding of the three aspects of Ezili that has come into my life.

Erzulie Freda/Erzulie Freda Dahomey is kind of like Aphrodite meets Barbie. She is the ultimate lady and likes to be treated as such. Erzulie Freda loves the fineries of womanhood, gold jewelry, makeup and fans... Not a fan of crass jokes and ungentlemanly actions, she seeks to bring love, prosperity and happiness to a person's life.

Erzulie Dantor is more like Aphrodite meets Khali. She can be that stern mother who can be overbearing and quite the task mistress however, may the good Lord watch out over anyone who trifles with anyone that Erzulie Dantor claims as a child. She is the consummate business woman and can manage all aspects of business from beginning to end. Remember though, with her dual daggers, Erzulie Dantor is ALSO a fighter extraordinaire taking on ANY and all challengers...

Then there is Erzulie Mapiang . Erzulie Mapiang is more like Aphrodite meets the Bag Lady. She may seem like a muttering, confused and homeless person however, she is the guardian of the homeless. Erzulie Mapiang is also the protectoress of anyone who has a disability or a mental handicap. Make no mistake, Erzulie Mapiang IS about love and the reason that SHE loves a person is that SHE knows they ARE NOT limited by what mere man thinks is a limitation.

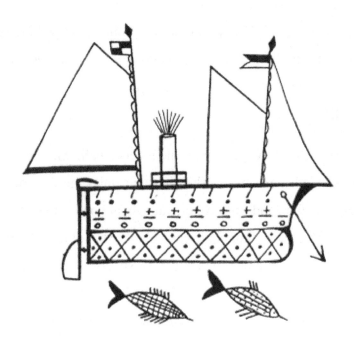

Veve for Papa Agwe

Papa Agwe

"Silent and strong, Agwe moves through the storms of our life, carrying us in his loving arms safely from shore to shore"… My Godmother used to say this when she would float a handmade, often more "strewn together" boat of drift wood, sticks and cloth for a sail. She was entreating Agwe to "ferry" us safely through the year and help us achieve our goals and desires. She would even float one of these makeshift boats as a representation of the dead being ferried across from the land of the living to "the other side" where they could heal and await to be reborn in a time when their energies were needed again.

Agwe is the husband of La Sirene and as such his domain is over the oceans and seas. Often considered the "Admiral" he is a boon to seafarers and fisherman alike. He is often sought to aid in sea travel, to fill the nets, to provide calm seas, to steer away storms (in conjunction with Oya) and to ferry messages to departed loved ones. Ceremonies for Agwe are generally conducted near water. His "Horse" will be washed and kept wet during the ceremony and people will be very conscious as Agwe will usually try to head towards the water. When giving Agwe offerings, they are often floated out to sea.

On Agwe's altar, you will find bits, baubles and more from the sea. One of the most special items will be a conch shell horn. In services to Agwe, this tool will be used to help summon him to your aid.

Veve for Papa Loko

Veve for Mama Ayizan

Papa Loko and Mama Ayizan

Papa Loko and Mama Ayizan were reputed to be the first Houngan (Priest) and Mambo (Priestess), according to what I was taught, with far reaching sight and a natural aptitude for the healing arts they were wise beyond years and worked in tandem to heal any and all sorts of wounds within their community.

Mama Ayizan was sought out for everything from fertility workings to major healing to fixing a broken heart. Papa Loko was often sought out for knowledge of magickal and healing herbs, protection, to right an injustice and to settle disputes...

Together, they are the forces sought out when one travels the priesthood within the Haitian traditions. Much of their works, world and being remain secret because of the need to protect the initiation process for Houngans and Mambos. What is known is that Papa Loko is the one who bestows the "Asson" (Holy rattle and bell) and Mama Ayizan is the one who "hosts" the initiation ceremonies.

I had a dream a few years ago and in it I could hear the sounds of a battle raging beyond my vision as I walked through a heavily forested area. Afraid. Intrigued. I slowly made my way through the forest and into a clearing. In the clearing stood a large tree with a canopy of leaves that sheltered people under it. Here, it was obvious that the fighting had not reached however, there were people running around and tending to wounded of all types.

I remember the scent of vanilla, jasmine and wild cinnamon in the air mixed with the coppery tang of blood from the wounded. A very distinctive aroma.

Walking closer, I noticed that the healers moving from person to person attempting to clean and bandage the wounds. As I peered closer I noticed that EACH healer had a distinctive tattoo on them... The tattoo was of snakeskin up one arm and varied butterflies down the other. So I looked at the wounded. Each of the wounded had markings depicting other Loa. Markings for Dantor, Ogun, Legba, the Ghede and more numbered among the fallen... It hurt my heart to see the carnage amongst the servants of the Loa...

I stopped one of the healers and asked them, "What has been happening? What has caused all of this?"... The one I had asked, merely answered, "Ask HIM." And pointed in the direction over my shoulder.

As I turned, I noted a large snake coming down a tree. When the large snake managed to slink to the bottom, it shifted to a beautiful dark-skinned man with pale blue eyes and snow white hair. He moved among the healers, touching their foreheads and whispering words in their ears. As he approached me, I noticed that he had a tattoo of a snake that started with the tip of its tail on the top of his foot, wrapping itself upward around his body, ending with the head of the snake following his left jaw line. Over his right eye, and in various locations showing his smooth, strongly muscled skin, were the tattoos of butterflies.

I stood awestruck at the man's beauty, his quiet assurance, his grace and his strength. Without so much as an offhanded glance, he strode straight to me. So. I asked again, "What has been happening? What has caused all of this?"

His answer scored me to my core. "The Children of Man are once again fighting over who has the right of it and who does not. Their pride is such that they cannot see that we have only given them pieces of the message so that they will work together to bring about the will of Olodumare."

With that, I awake and have a whole new respect for the path that I have been traveling for so long.

The Ghede and the Dead

In every form of Voodoo, whether it is Haitian Vodou, Louisiana Voodoo, New Orleans Voodoo, or any of the other Diaspora, you will find a loving reverence of the dead that borders almost on worship. Indeed, the way the dead are treated is more respectful than many other more "acceptable" religions (as many of the more nature oriented religions will). They are honored, offered libations and even fed their favorite foods (when such things are known, such as whatever Grandma So-N-So's favorite food may have been). There is even a specific day of the week that they are honored, let alone what is done for their birthdays, known anniversaries, and more.

Many in New Orleans Voodoo will have a specific pot (mine is a cast iron cauldron put together for me by my first Godmother made with dirt from cemeteries containing my family) that is used to represent their resting place in your home. Working with the dead becomes almost second nature because it is believed that they are still, spiritually, around waiting on a call from us for them to come help us accomplish deeds and goals in our lives. Work may be done at your own altars, at crossroads, OR at a cemetery and it will ALWAYS be done in the utmost respect (this means you WILL clean up your mess and not leave things such as broken glass behind).

In the process of dealing with your dead, you will also find "The Ancestors" and their guardian spirits, The Ghede (geh-DEH). The Ghede are part of the Loa tree of Spirits one will deal with in New Orleans Voodoo and come by way of the Haitian traditions brought into the New Orleans tradition. There is a truly diverse set of Spirits within the Ghede pantheon. Baron Samedi, Baron la Cemetrie, Baron la Croix, Baron Criminal, Papa Ghede, Ghede Nibo, Mama Brigitte and so many more. The ones that I've particularly dealt with are Baron Samedi, Papa Ghede, Mama Brigitte and Ghede Nibo.

Baron Samedi (Baron Saturday) is treated, in the tradition that I learned, as the "Father (or Chief) of the Ghede Spirits". Due to his being the "Father of the Ghede Spirits", he stands at the ultimate crossroad, that crossroad that stands between life and death. He leads the dead from this life to the next life and is responsible for the making and breaking of magicks in a person's life. Often he is sought out for the simple comfort of knowing that our dearly departed are safe and looked after. Baron Samedi is often portrayed as a gaunt, nearly skeletal, man in a tuxedo (some say with tails), a cane used more as a walking stick than for an ailment, a top hat (usually beat up a bit) and a pair of sunglasses (usually with the left lens popped out). He tends to "stroll" instead of jaunt through when he makes his appearances in dreams. When riding a person, that

114

person usually becomes rigid (as with rigor mortis) and a form of mumbling speech takes over. Often times another priest or priestess will be ridden by yet another Ghede to translate for the Baron.

Mama Brigitte is an entertaining spirit. Much like many "motherly" spirits, she represents the mothers who have crossed over and is FIERCELY protective of children and the spirits of children who have passed away. Often her personal veve resembles the tree with which she is associated, the Weeping Willow. This is said to be a holdover from her days as a Celtic Goddess who wept over her own son's death. Often portrayed in a bridal gown, Mama Brigitte is caring and warm until you get on her bad side... Think of the worst attacks by bears and lions you can think of and imagine it multiplied by 50... Indeed, many of the Ghede Spirits are HIGHLY protective of children.

The Dead themselves, termed "ghede" with a lower case 'g' in New Orleans Voodoo, are honored and treated with the utmost dignity and respect, as they are in many ATRs and their offshoots. These are our Ancestors, our forbearers, which include those that we pay homage to who, in order to continue their much loved traditions, had to hide their practices from the often overzealous eyes of the overseers. These people, in New Orleans Voodoo, become an honored part of the tradition that is often celebrated and thanked throughout every major celebration we hold. We acknowledge their sacrifice DAILY in how we wear our eleke. Our tradition is to wear a rosary outside (or in front of) our eleke to signify our acknowledgement of how our Ancestors had to hide their spirituality from the prying eyes of those who would disdain it or, through their lack of understanding and fear, attempt to stamp it out altogether.

The Ghede

In New Orleans style of Voodoo, I am considered "Ghede bound". This means that I deal with the dead in all of their places and is a nod to the abilities and capabilities of the Spirits that make up the family of Ghede. Like many of the families within the pantheon of Spirits that are the Loa, there are many Ghede Spirits.

Baron Samedi, according to how I was trained, is the chief of the Ghede Spirits and is, along with his wife and son, the ultimate judge of situations. When you go to them, you MUST make sure that your own nose is clean.

The Ghede Spirits are said to be the "makers and breakers of all magick" and when you go to their resting places, you can be sure that whatever magick has been placed on you, or that you need to be placed on something else, WILL get done. Magicks and respect are generally done at the oldest tomb in a cemetery OR the tomb of your dearly beloved who has sloughed off this mortal coil. Offerings often entail favorite foods of your departed family members, candy, rum, cigars, raw beef and even hot peppers.

Rituals for healing, love, cleansing, money, protection, destruction of fears, defeat of an enemy and so much more can be done when working with the Ghede Spirits, whether it is Baron Samedi, his brothers Barons Cemetrie and La Croix, his wife, Mama Brigitte and his son, Papa Ghede.

Just remember to be respectful when dealing with the dead in their "cities" and that ALL cemeteries (cities of the dead) are connected. This means, that when you walk in one, you walk in all.

One thing that we do, here in New Orleans, when entering a cemetery is to cross ourselves three times while facing outward and walk in backwards, at least, three steps. When leaving the cemeteries, we merely reverse the process. Face inwards, cross yourself three times and then back out again three steps… It was done this way so that you did not bring anything disrespectful into the cemeteries with you and so that nothing, inadvertently, followed you out of the cemeteries to your home.

New Orleans own "Loa"; Queen Marie Laveau

There is one other Spiritual Force that plays a HUGE part in New Orleans style of Voodoo. This Spiritual Force took the form of a particular woman that has been active since the very day of her birth as a "Free Woman of Color" in 1801 in the beautiful city of New Orleans. I am talking about the one and only, Marie Laveau. For those of us who practice Voodoo in the New Orleans tradition, there is but one person who made it truly possible for us to practice our religion openly in and around the New Orleans area.

Marie was known as several things. She was a "procuress" and could get pretty much anything anyone ever needed. Whether it was a simple tromp through the swamps to find and acquire an item needed for some working or a person for someone to marry. Often times these people were bought OUT of slavery so that they could marry freely. Marie was also a consummate business woman. She made decisions that affected her business on a daily basis. As a hair dresser, she was privy to all the gossip of the city and, through rumor and speculation of course, she could move throughout the city and handle business as it came up.

An example of this can be seen in the passing of the "Tignon Law". It is said that in the 1800s white women were becoming jealous of the many new and fantastic hairstyles of the African and African American women that incorporated pretty trinkets and jewels in them. They were hard pressed to find a way to stop these new changes and spoke of it often... A few influential ladies made their way to Marie Laveau's hair salon to get their hair done and began to speak, as often happens, in front of the hair dresser. Thinking quickly, Marie Laveau suggested that African women used to wrap their heads in what was often called a tignon.

Thinking that making the black women cover their head would be a great idea to stop the beautiful and bejeweled hairstyles that they were always creating, the white women had their husbands pass the law... WITHOUT doing any true research on what a tignon really was.

Tignons became the new hairstyles made of brightly colored and bejeweled clothes and stacked high upon the heads of women of color throughout New Orleans thus thwarting the jealous actions of a few jealous women. As it had been made into a law that women of color could not move throughout the city without their hair being covered, there was nothing they could do.

This just ONE of the ways that Marie Laveau had influenced policies in the city.

Marie Laveau and Pere Antoine, a Spanish Friar who presided over St Louis Cathedral, would often be seen together moving from hospice to hospital to prison ministering to everyone from the sick and infirm to those sentenced to life and/or death in prison. It is rumored, and as I wasn't personally there, I can only report it as such, that Marie Laveau and Pere Antoine struck a bargain so that Voodoo practitioners could practice without the persecution of the Church. The story states that she approached Pere Antoine and swore to keep his pews full if he and the Church would leave them to their ceremonies. The bargain was struck and Marie was good at her word which made working with her that much easier for Pere Antoine. The pair worked closely for many years because of this.

Each year, Marie Laveau held a ceremony on Bayou St John for St John's Eve, which is continued to this day by practitioners even now. People would travel from all over the world to participate in one of Marie Laveau's St John's Eve ceremonies.

From ceremonies in Congo Square to hair dressing to influencing political views and agendas, Mama Marie Laveau was TRULY and excellent resource for the practitioner in and around the New Orleans area. Because of this, the works she did and more, she was considered by OTHERS to be a Queen of Voodoo. She did not claim the title herself, it was bestowed upon her by those who believed in her and continues, to this day, to be a viable and apt description of the woman who made it possible for everything we are able to do today.

The very fact that her spirit continues to be an active resource in the Crescent City is why many practitioners consider her New Orleans own "Loa". People come to New Orleans from around the world to visit the tomb of Marie Laveau in St Louis #1, leaving her offerings and beseeching her on behalf of some need. It is an amazing thing to see just how many people come to her…

A simple reminder

The list of Orisha and Loa that I have provided are simply a small portion of the potential Spirits that one can come to know in this great adventure that many of us have already begun. There are several that I haven't even begun to scratch the surface of myself and I am constantly learning new things about the ones I deal with on a regular basis. There are many different offshoots of the African Traditional Religions and finding one that feels right to AND for you will be a journey that can make it all worthwhile.

Remember that your journey with the Orisha and the Loa are just that… YOUR journey and they will meet you half-way in all of your endeavors. They will help you grow into the person you and Olodumare/God has in store for you…

Veve for the Marassa

Les Morte/Our Ancestors

Throughout virtually every tradition stemming from the ATRs, you will find that the Ancestors, our Revered Dead, will be honored. It is a way of keeping traditions alive, remembering where we came from, the people who came before, what they went through, the things they learned and so much more. Much of the time, Ancestral Reverie is seen as a collection of odd little items surrounding wooden or plastic skeletons, skulls, small ceramic and wooden coffins, Statues of St Expedite, token reminders of those you've lost in your life and more.

It is believed that, even though the Dead (Les Morte/The Ancestors) no longer have a physical body that they have not completely moved on from this realm yet. They are still helping us, still endeavoring to help us and, put simply, are waiting for us to call on them to help us during our times of trouble. For this reason, we honor them. For this reason we continue to treat them with dignity and respect throughout our walk with God/Olodumare/Bondye.

The way that my original Godmother explained this to me is that, since the Dead no longer have a physical body, they don't have the same restrictions that we have when approaching God. They now exist on the same plane and can communicate with him, on our behalf, directly. "No middleman" as my God mother used to say.

Altars for the dead in my home started out very Spartan because I simply didn't want them imposing themselves any more into my life than they already did... Since traveling this path and setting my footing in the Priesthood, I've developed an easier rapport with them and my altar has grown to show this. My altar has become a connection to my Mother, Grandmother, Grandfathers and anyone else who was precious to me that have joined the Silent Majority (to borrow a term from one of my favorite book series)...

The Convergence Begins

If you recall, I wrote that New Orleans style of Voodoo is a combinative belief system. This shows more in the fact that where we used to hide behind Catholicism, we have now truly embraced and incorporated it into our practices. Root workers of EVERY imagined manner call on the intercessors for the Divine Almighty for everything from simple trials to complex endeavors of attraction. I will list off several of the Catholic Saints with whom I have personally dealt with and their prayers, along with reasons as to why I have called on them just to give you an idea of how integrated these Spirits have become into today's Voodoo. I have also taken the time to list their day of celebration so that those serious seekers out there may begin to take their journey and make it a little bit easier on you. Easier than it was for me in the beginning, anyways...

Before I begin, I would like to relate to you how this section came into being. For a while, this book had virtually slowed to a crawl... I could get a few lines out, here and there, at a time and just could not for the life of me figure out what was going on. I began to question what was missing; why the book didn't have the flow that it originally felt when I began. I could tell that something was amiss; I just couldn't tell what it was. In the course of an evening, when I was becoming absolutely flustered and frustrated by the lack of flow from something that I KNEW Spirit had impressed upon me to write, I called out to Spirit to help me (finally... Isn't always that way though?). My two cats, Eshu (my own little trickster) and Ashanti Rose were playing near my Ghede altar in my bedroom some 4 feet away from the bookcase where I have my collection of Voodoo/Vodou, Santeria, Ifa and other knowledge from the myriad of attempts to present "anthropological" views... During the course of their mock battle, a book hit the floor between the two of them in such a way that the three of us jumped... When I looked at the book, it was the most amazing "DUH!" moment I think I have ever had in my life... There, on the floor in front of us, was a book entitled "Cooking with the Saints"!!!

That was it. THAT was what was missing from the book. I've written about some of the Orisha. I've written about some of the Loa. However. I had written NOTHING about the Saints that they are synchronized with. I had forgotten the "Cross-over" section. What makes the ATROs their own separate, legitimate experiences.

Like I said... It was the most amazing "DUH!" moment I think I have ever had in my life.

The African Side with a twist

This particular section of the book is concerned with the synchronization of the Catholic Saints and the African and, sometimes, the Loa. Just as with the section of this title, each of the

Orisha I have named are a family of Spirits that aid in our daily lives as God is overseeing the entirety of the universe. This is coming from the traditions that I was taught by my Godmother, corroborated by the Haitian traditions that I am still in the process of learning.

Monnot's St Peter

St Peter (June 29)

St Peter is often called on as a "Crossroad's Spirit" as he was synchronized with the Ellegua family of Spirits (Ellegua/Papa Legba/Eshu). Prayers are offered to him to open doors, close doors properly and aid in forward movement in life. We will also offer prayers to him when there is a serious decision to be made which could have an unknown outcome on our lives so that it will be shifted to the more favorable or desired outcome. St Peter is also called upon for strength and forgiveness.

Glorious King of the Apostles to whom our Lord, Jesus Christ, spoke first after his glorious and wonderful resurrection. We beg you to grant us the grace that the Lord designated you to give us, and for the intimate thoughts of your conscience. To think about us poor people and forgive us our faults, Glorious Saint Peter, and grant us this grace so that we can purify our souls by means of true pain and cleanse ourselves of everything that has offended you. Grant that by the help of this intercession, we may be released from the bonds of our sins. Amen

Image of St Michael

Saint Michael the Archangel(Sept 29)

St Michael the Archangel is another Spirit synchronized to the Ellegua family of Spirits. In some traditions, St Michael is also affiliated with and/or synchronized with the Ogun family of Spirits. In New Orleans Voodoo, St Michael is associated with BOTH Spirits. He is called on in times of worry when our strength is sorely lacking and we feel that there may just be some sort of enmity at work in our lives. Whether this enmity comes from acts of jealousy or malicious intent doesn't really matter, St Michael will take it all on. We will also call on him as a "Communicator Spirit" as he is one of the many Angels that bear messages from God to the faithful (and sometimes those who may have lost their faith or never had it to begin with)...

Prayer 1: **Saint Michael the Archangel, defend us in the day of battle and be our safeguard against the wickedness and snares of the devil. We humbly pray, by the power of God, cast into hell, Satan and all other evil spirits, who prowl through the world, seeking the ruin of souls. Amen****

Prayer 2: ** Saint Michael the Archangel, as you are the person in charge of all the works in the world, I implore you at this solemn hour and day, seize this time so that you will see the light, candle and work. Come sorcery and corruption and revoke yourselves in my body. The flesh and blood of my enemy should treat me well.

Let my enemies suffer as Jesus suffered on the Cross, bitterness, torment, kicks and slaps

Let him go into a desolate world. Let him take the three falls that Jesus took until he comes to my home asking pardon for his sins. The stars in Heaven bear witness to my pleas. So be it. Amen****

Image for St George

Saint George (April 23)

St George is one of the Saints associated with and synchronized to the Spiritual family of the Ogun tree (Ogun/Ogou Badagris/Ogou St Jacques/Ogou Ferray) and, as such, is revered as a warrior of distinction. When marshalling the forces of Good to surround you, it is often necessary to call on St George (Ogun). Now this marshalling of the forces of Good can be for simple protection to breaking bad habits to even more dangerous admonitions of ill intent...

Prayer 1: ****Powerful Lord, example of the humble, you defended us from the vices of the demon with your lance, to bring us to Heaven. Through your humbleness, glorious Martyr Saint George, we humbly ask for your intercession and victory over dangers which afflict us. We**

will achieve a haven of happiness after our trials and tribulations. We shall pass safely through life, and then praise you in Heaven. Amen.**

Prayer 2: ***Powerful knight, example to the humble, you defend us from vices with your lance, and also from the Devil, in order to transport us to glory. By the humility of God's glorious martyr, Saint George, we humbly ask for the efficacious intercession of the saint to defeat all the dangers that sadden my existence, helping me anchor at a joyous port when fatigued, and to safely navigate the crossing over to glory, where I may eternally sing your praises. Amen***

Image of Santa Barbara

Saint Barbara (Dec 4)

St Barbara (more often pronounced "Santa Barbara" by local practitioners) is synchronized to the Orisha Chango/Shango/Xango and is sought in matters of conflict, whether that is simply needing a Warrior Spirit to fight for you or a "Defensive Spirit" to go to bat for you in matters of a legal nature.

Prayer 1: ***Oh God, keep away from me all those malicious and miserable beings who would stalk me. I seek you out, St Barbara, so you may confound them. Keep them at bay, and as I call upon you, offering my heart and life to you, divine Christian maiden whose bosom is welcoming to all good beings, cleanse me with your martyr's blood so that those who attempt to do evil to me will end up in Hell. Amen.** (this prayer is generally followed by three Our Fathers and three Hail Marys)*

Prayer 2: *** Magnificent and eternal God, we admire your Saints, especially the glorious Virgin and the Martyr Saint Barbara. We give thanks for those who were worthy of your intercession and were freed from all evil, helping them in their hour of need, not permitting them to die without receiving the Holy Sacraments, and granting them and assuring them that their petitions had been heard. I beg everything by the merits of the dear Saint Barbara.*

Give me strength to resist all temptations and to know my faults. And so to be worthy of that sacred and Holy Virgin, especially in my hour of death, fortified with the Holy Sacraments and by them and the intercession of Saint Barbara, happy in your company

with you and with your glory, where you live and reign in Heaven.
Amen. ***

Saint Therese (Oct 1)

As one of the Saints associated with the Orisha Oya, St Therese is often sought to invoke change, aid in business/scholastic endeavors, and to honor your Ancestors.

** My Lord and my God, I have realized that whoever undertakes to do anything for the sake of earthly things or to earn praise of others deceives himself. Today on thing pleases the world,

tomorrow another. What is praised on one occasion is denounced on another. Blessed be You, my Lord and my God, for You are unchangeable for all eternity. Whoever serves You faithfully to the end will enjoy life without end in eternity. Amen.** (this prayer always reminded me of just how fickle the "Winds of Change" can be...)

Our Lady of Candlemas (personal choice)(Feb 2)

Often when dealing with Oya in her aspect of being the "Queen of the Winds and Hurricanes" I have added this prayer when invoking changes in my life. Again. This is MERELY a personal choice to add her in my workings with Oya and her energies. It is also good to note that this particular prayer calls on a, seemingly, little known quality of Oya... Like many of the African Spirit Forces, she too is a Warrior Spirit...

** Welcome, Oh Queen of Heaven. Welcome, Oh Lady of Angels. Hail! Thou root, hail! Thou gate from within unto the world, a light has arisen: rejoice, Oh glorious Virgin, lovely beyond all others, farewell, most beautiful maiden, and pray for us to Christ our Lord.

Allow me to praise thee, Oh sacred Virgin!

Against mine enemies give me strength!

138

Grant unto us, Oh Merciful God, a defense against our weakness, that we, who remember the holy Mother of our Lord and Savior, by the help of her intercession, may rise from our iniquities, through the same Christ our Lord. Amen.**

Statue of Our Lady of Mercy (Mother of Mercy)

Our Lady of Mercy (Mother of Mercy)(Sept 24)

Associated with the Orisha, Obatala, Our Lady of Mercy is often sought out in matters of health, balance, and spiritual cleansing. She is also sought in matters of addiction and anytime you feel "shackled" to a negative source up to and including "liberation" or freedom.

**Blessed Virgin Mary, who can worthily repay you with praise and thanks for having rescued a fallen world by your generous consent! Receive our gratitude, and by your prayers obtain the pardon of our sins. Take our prayers into the sanctuary of heaven and enable them to make our peace with God.*

*Holy Mary, help the miserable, strengthen the discouraged, comfort the sorrowful, pray for your people, plead for the clergy, intercede for all women consecrated to God. May all who venerate you feel now your help and protection. Be ready to help us when we pray, and bring back to us the answers to our prayers. Make it your continual concern to pray for the people of God, for you were blessed by God and were made worthy to bear the Redeemer of the world, who lives and reigns forever. Amen.***

Saint

Mother of Charity (Our Lady of Charity)

Mother of Charity (Sept 8)

Synchronized to the African Orisha, Oshun, the Mother of Charity
is often called on by people seeking not only love but prosperity of
a personal nature, as well. When all seems lost and you are looking
at the "poorest" time of your life, turn to Mother of Charity for the
hope that is so desperately needed. This could even be done during

times of illness. "Poor" in this sense is based on how you feel it means to you.

Oh, Holy Virgin and Lady of Charity, with happiness and humility, I come to your feet!

Virgin of Miracles! You cure the sick, you give hope where there is only despair, you give strength to the afflicted, preserve our family from disgrace, protect the youth, guard our children.

No one can explain the miracles and fortitude you give to the souls that come to you.

*We, your children, thank you for all your graces. Amen.***

Image for Mary- Star of the Sea

Mary – Star of the Sea (September 27)

Associated and synchronized to the African Orisha, Yemaya, Mary-Star of the Sea (Stella Maris) is sought in endeavors ranging from the simple protections of a loving mother to protection of those whose livelihood revolves around the sea (fishermen, navy, coast guard, etc) to matters of fertility/child birth/child rearing to prosperity for the whole home.

Hail, O Bright Star of the ocean, God's own Mother blest, ever sinless Virgin, gate of heav'nly rest.

Taking that sweet Ave, which from Gabriel came, peace confirm within us, changing Eve's name.

Break the sinners' fetters, make our blindness day, Chase all evils from us, for all blessings pray.

Show thyself a Mother, may the Word divine born for us thine Infant hear our prayers through thine.
Virgin all excelling, mildest of the mild, free from guilt preserve us meek and undefiled.

Keep our life all spotless, make our way secure till we find in Jesus, joy for evermore.

Praise to God the Father, honor to the Son, in the Holy Spirit, be the glory one.

Amen.

Image of Our Lady of Regla

Our Lady or Regla (Sept 8)

Associated and also synchronized to the African Orisha, Yemaya, Our Lady of Regla is seen holding a child as a testament to her prowess as a mother. Often sought for issues of motherhood from conception to post natal care, she is also another one to go to when for everything from healing to prosperity of your home.

Our Lady of Regla, Mother of Divine Graces and source of our happiness, I beg for your powerful intercession. You are the

145

keeper of divine grace. The Most High has made you the dispenser of all His power in heaven and on earth. The numerous miracles that God has performed on your behalf prove that you are the remedy for all our ills and comfort in our sorrows. At this hour I beg of your goodness. Obtain for me the source of all grace, and the grace I now seek: _____. May I live and die worthy of enjoying the happiness of heaven with you. Amen.**

The Haitian Side

Image of St Patrick

St Patrick (March 17th)

Synchronized to the Spirit Damballah, St Patrick is often called upon for good fortune in travel, breaking the bonds of addiction, liberation and healing.

May the Strength of God pilot us.
May the Power of God preserve us.
May the Wisdom of God instruct us.
May the Hand of God protect us.
May the Way of God direct us.
May the Shield of God defend us.
May the Host of God guard us.
Against the snares of the evil ones.
Against temptations of the world

May Christ be with us!
May Christ be before us!
May Christ be in us,
Christ be over all!
May Thy Salvation, Lord,
Always be ours,
This day, O Lord, and evermore. Amen.

Image of St Joseph

Saint Joseph (March 19)

Associated with Papa Loko in the Haitian Traditions, St Joseph is often sought out for protection (in particular the protection of children) and guidance. He is also sought in times when physical, strenuous labor is necessary to accomplish a task to help ease the burden of the task so that the labor comes to fruition without hindrances.

Here, in New Orleans, Saint Joseph's Day is a huge celebration featuring altars with lavishly decorated and baked loaves of bread. Foods prepared for Saint Joseph's Day are generally shared with "strangers" and your home opened to those who may have become estranged in your lives, in the hopes of reestablishing the connections that once were there.

As an aside... St Joseph is also sought out by those wishing to find or sell a home... There's even a complete feast with prayers that you can do to aid this.

Prayer 1

O Blessed Saint Joseph, faithful guardian and protector of virgins, to whom God entrusted Jesus and Mary, I implore you by the love which you did bear them, to preserve me from every defilement of soul and body, that I may always serve them in holiness and purity of love. Amen.

Prayer 2 (used to ask for protection of children)

O glorious St. Joseph,
to you God committed the care
of His only begotten Son
amid the many dangers of this world.
We come to you
and ask you to take under your special protection
the children God has given us.
Through holy baptism they became children of God
and members of His holy Church.
We consecrate them to you today,
that through this consecration
they may become your foster children.

Guard them, guide their steps in life,

form their hearts after the hearts of Jesus and Mary.

St. Joseph,

who felt the tribulation and worry of a parent

when the child Jesus was lost,

protect our dear children for time and eternity.

May you be their father and counselor.

let them, like Jesus,

grow in age as well as in wisdom

and grace before God and men.

Preserve them from the corruption of this world,

and give us the grace one day

to be united with them in heaven forever.

Amen.

Image of St Isidore the Farmer

Saint Isidore the Farmer (May 15)

Associated with Cousin Azaka (Kuzan Zaka), St Isidore is the boon of the working man or woman. Sought in labor disputes, when you are owed money for actual work done (let's be honest, some people think they are owed money while sitting on their backsides instead of doing the job they were hired to do) and when you are the owner of a business and you are needing to light a fire under your employees, St Isidore is the ultimate go to guy for these issues. He is also sought in issues of farming and gardening to make sure that harvests are plentiful and that the crops grow properly.

Image of St Ulrich

Saint Ulrich (July 14)

In the world of Voodoo/Vodou, St Ulrich is associated with the Loa, Agwe, the Husband of the ever beautiful, La Siren. Often sought out to care for naval oriented military personnel, such as the Navy and Coast Guard, he also is a boon to ANYONE who makes a living on the Seas and Oceans. Between St Ulrich and Diosa Del Mar (Agwe and La Siren), the bounty of the Seas are available for those who work well with the Spirits who govern them.

Father, you are rich in mercy;
in a time of severe hardship
you sent your people
the energetic Bishop St Ulrich.
We ask you, through his prayers,
to weather the dangers and perils
of our present times
by the strength and power of our Faith.
Through our Lord Jesus Christ, your Son,
who lives and reigns with you
in the unity of the Holy Spirit,
one God, for ever and ever.
Amen.

Image of Diosa del Mar

Synchronization extended

I think it is important to denote that in New Orleans traditional Voodoo, the idea of synchronization has extended itself into "spheres of influence", as well. Each Orisha and Loa are seen to influence certain aspects of our world, all the while reminding us that those spheres may overlap and even converge. I will endeavor to remind you, however, that this is NOT the way of most of the traditions. In most of the traditions, you can go to your particular Spirits for practically any purpose. Even in New Orleans Voodoo, this is a trend, however, it is taught that each has their area of expertise that they are more capable of helping with.

Remember that EACH Orisha and Loa can, ultimately, help you with any endeavor, however, I will place what I was taught here for a "Go To" guide, should you feel the need to go for specialized attentions.

Ellequa/Papa Lebga/Eshu: These Spirits of the Cross Roads

How to make a gris gris bag/mojo hand

Here I thought I would take the time to tell you all how I, personally, make a gris gris bag. The color of the bag depends on the working that you are attempting and everyone sees the color coordination for purposes differently:

My personal list follows along this line:

Love: red or pink cloth/purple yarn

Strength: red cloth/red yarn

Healing: light blue cloth/white or light blue yarn

Spiritual Cleansing: white cloth/white or silver yarn

Peace: white cloth/dark blue yarn

Money: green cloth/yellow or gold yarn

Good Luck: yellow or gold cloth/green or gold yarn

Protection: black cloth/white yarn

Destruction of Fear: black cloth/black yarn

Draw love: white or red cloth/red or pink yarn

These are just some of the various gris gris bags/mojo hands that I have made for others.

In a bowl, you are going to mix the herbal ingredients which matches your desired task for the gris gris bag. Saying whatever prayer work or Psalm you equate with the purpose (a good reference point would be "The Psalm Workbook" by Robert Laremy/Original Publications) while mixing the herbal ingredients together. If you feel like it, you can add a few drops of an oil that coincides with the purpose you are creating the gris gris bag for and continue to mix for a little longer.

Have a 4 inch by 4 inch square of cloth ready (it can be bigger for those of you who may have issues with the smaller size however I wouldn't make it too much smaller than 4X4) so that when you are done mixing you can stuff your gris gris bag.

While laying the square swatch of cloth over the palm of one hand, curl your palm and push the cloth down to fit this new "bowl" shape. Reach into your mix and pull out a good sized "pinch" of mixture. Place this in your newly formed "bowl". Do this a couple of times to insure a good fill.

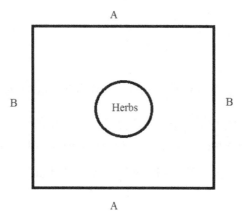

Pull up the "A" opposite sides to begin to form a wall. Repeat with the remaining "B" sides. Grab the bag closer to the collection of herbs so that it forms a ball of a sort. With your other hand, begin to wrap your corresponding yarn, leaving you enough at the start to tie to some at the end. Tie the ends together as tight as your yarn will allow.

Recite any closing prayer or Psalm that you choose to lock in the energy. Women should carry the newly created device on their left side. Men should carry it on their right side.

That's it in a nutshell. How to make a gris gris bag/mojo hand as I do it.

How to make a Voodoo Doll!!!

As a reminder, there is no set in stone rule as to how to precisely make a Voodoo Doll. Many people will make the stick and moss doll because they are relatively simple to make. However, I am a "stitch doll" kind of person and tend to use a pattern to create dolls that I simply stitch together by hand. The key thing to remember when assembling a doll is that the doll, itself, will become the representative of your desire. IT becomes the love you crave, the money you wish to draw to you, the health you are searching for and/or the protection that you require. It does not matter if you are doing these things for yourself or for another person. The doll becomes the focal tool to bring about these desired changes in your life.

For you to create a doll, you merely need to focus on the type of doll you are creating and begin its construction. Recited whatever prayers you would like (New Orleans Voodoo practitioners generally use the Psalms along with prayers to specific Saints and Orisha that might be over the particular need)

A good list of Psalms to use for practical application is:

Love: 33, 88, 111 & 148

Healing: 3, 19, 30, 49, 89, 102 & 127 (89 is a particular favorite of my family)

Money & Good Luck: 21, 65, 73, 92, 108, 113 & 132

Protection: 4, 23, 24, 46, 91 & 121

Spiritual Cleansing: 40, 61, 85 & 138

Fertility: 98, 102, 103 & 127
Goodbye Foe/Enemy Be Gone: 28, 35, 79, 94, 110, 112 & 145

For a more specific list of the Psalms and what they can be used for, you can check out each section of work that I've added to this book.

A good basic pattern for a doll can be found pretty much anywhere online or by visiting a craft shop or fabric store. For the sake of simplicity (see what I did there??) I will add one here. This pattern can be copied from the book, expanded and made to the size you feel you wish to create.

Take the time to figure out whether you or going to make your doll with filler or if you are going to ONLY use herbs, roots and oils. It

162

is important to note, that if you are simply using the herbs, roots and oils that you may wish to make a smaller doll, depending on which herb you are using as your primary filler.

Generally speaking, when I am making a Voodoo Doll of the stitch variety, I will make a sachet of the herbs, roots and oils to place in the center of the doll as its "heart" and fill the rest with some other filler, such as the filler you can buy to fill pillows.

It is up to each reader as to which herbs they feel represents the needs they desire. I do have specific herbs that I will use for specific projects however, there are literally dozens of books out there on which herbs work with what purpose. Make sure to take into account any allergies you or your perspective recipient may have and work around those.

Example: If you are working a love doll and you or the person you are working the doll for are allergic to roses, you will not want to add them to the doll. Common sense and practicality should play a role in what you are attempting to do.

A good book to find magickal properties of herbs is "Encyclopedia of Magical Herbs" by Scott Cunningham (Llewellyn Publications). Check the back appendices for a breakdown of what herbs work for what magickal need. (More precisely, pages 276-284)

Each section will contain instructions on the specific creation of a doll for that general purpose... Yes it will read much as a repeat however, I feel that it is important to show that MUCH of Voodoo workings ARE repetitive and simplistic in nature. There are some VERY famous works that are so simple, you really have to admire just how simple they are.

"Nothing is done without the eyes of God." ~ An old Haitian Vodou Saying

The next pages that you will read is technically a cross between Hoodoo and Voodoo, however, the easy to remember thing is that Voodoo always ritualizes things. There is ALWAYS a ceremony when it comes to Voodoo. Hoodoo gets down and dirty into the magick because it didn't have the Saints of Catholicism to hide behind.

I should state here, for the record, that there is a vast difference between HAVING faith and USING faith. Having faith, everyone does this. Everyone acknowledges the fact that "I have faith" or "I believe that God will intervene on my behalf" or something like this. USING faith, however, is quite different. When a Voodoo practitioner begins a work, they KNOW that the work is going to work. There is no second guessing. There is no doubt. We simply trust that it is going to happen. Even when the answer by God is "No," we trust that the work WILL work in a way that God has chosen for us.

Having faith will say, "I hope this magick will work."

Using faith will say, "I know this magick will work."

When you do this work; when you BEGIN this work, KNOW that these will aid you in gaining your desires. So I say to you, now, USE FAITH. Practice faith daily. Make your connection to the Divine Creative Source; to God/Olodumare/Bondye STONG so that NO ONE can shake it. EVER.

Now we get to move on to the fun informative stuff that you've probably been waiting for my verbose backside to get to.

Spiritual Cleansing

I figured that I would start this section of the book, the "tricks" section of the book, with something that is a staple in Voodoo (using Voodoo as a "umbrella" term here folks) practices of all types... Spiritual Cleansing.

In practically every religious belief on the face of the planet, there is a form of Spiritual Cleansing that can and, indeed, must be accomplished from time to time in order of our world to move forward, free us from blockages, and remove negative energy/emotions/intent from our lives. New Orleans style of Voodoo is no different. We have a few things we do, in order to cleanse a person based on the severity of what we feel their case represents. These Spiritual Cleansings range from simple smudges to baths to a full out "exorcism". All of which are designed to remove the negative influence from your life allowing you to move into your future without distraction or attachment...

To this end, I have compiled a few of my favorite methods here, allowing a bit more access to something that others may not quite understand nor be able to find themselves.

I should note here… NO work is done without first entreating Ellegua/Papa Legba. It is imperative that either of these Spirits are first called upon and saluted or the other Spirits you call on may deem the working "not proper" and choose to stay away from it. This can be done by saying a simple prayer, lighting up Ellegua's/Papa Legba's altar, and pouring libations near the door to entice him to aid in your work.

Spiritual Cleansing:

In New Orleans Voodoo, we generally call on Obatala or Papa Damballa to aid in cleansing unwanted or negative energies from a person, adding in a call to Oya to help provide the necessary change and transition from unwanted energy to wanted and negative energy to positive. So, the general way this would go…

1) Open the doors by calling/singing/praying to Ellegua/Papa Legba

2) Pour libations at the door to entice Spirit to join in your working

3) Call on Oya to aid in the transition work (Generally, I use the song "Oya Mi Do" to facilitate in this).

4) Call on Obatala or Damballa to cleanse away the unwanted/negative energy.

5) Smudge/Bathe the person you are removing the energies from

6) Use something such as Florida Water or some other agent of your choosing to "lock in" the positive intention of your Cleansing Ritual.

7) Close out by giving thanks to each Spirit you called on, thanks to God/Olodumare/Bondye for His help in allowing this energy to be removed.

(This is a good example of ANY ritual you may be planning, if you want to be honest. Just remember to give thanks to EACH Spirit you call on in your work when closing out. It pays to honor them all, no matter what the working, so that they continue to listen to your calls...)

A good list of Psalms to aid in this venture are:

Cleanse a Jinx/Curse/Hex: 7, 10, 29, 38, 69 & 110

Cleanse a person (general): 68

Cleanse an "evil spirit": 10, 15, 24 & 91

Cleanse an Unknown negativity: 40, 61, 85 & 138

Spiritual Cleansing Smudges:

Smudge 1: This smudge is a simple resin or herb mix burnt over charcoal and used to "bathe" the person needing cleansed. During these times, you would start the smudge at the top of the person's head, working COUNTER clockwise from that point around the body in an outline to "cut the ties" and then begin circling the body with the smoking mixture, moving down the body to remove negative influences, energies or intents.

Commonly used resins and herbs (try out several to see which combination works best for you) include, but are not limited to: gum copal, black copal, frankincense and myrrh, dragon's blood, rosemary, cedar and pinion pine. (Note: I did not list sage here for the reason I listed earlier in this book.)

Smudge 2: Using white and purple chord, tie together these three dried ingredients while reciting Psalm 23 a total of 7 times: rosemary, cedar and sage. Light this bundle and, again, beginning at the top of the head of the person being cleansed. Move the smoking bundle counter clockwise around the person in an outline form (like you were cutting out a paper doll). When you come back to the top of the head, begin to smudge down the body.

Bath 1: Combine these ingredients (generally the herbs are to be 2-3 tablespoons and oils by the dram however, like many things; you can fiddle with this to suit your own needs, money, and time)...

Dry herbs: rosemary, cedar, juniper berries, cascarilla (crushed), red sandalwood, rose and sage

Liquid ingredients: rosemary, sage, camphor and cedar, 7 ounce bottle of Florida Water and 2 cups of hot water.

While mixing these ingredients together in a large pot/bowl or other container, recite Psalm 23 a total of 7 times. This insures that God's hand is in the working. Run a bath without any other additives, making it as hot as you prefer. Add the mixture and recite Psalm 23 one time.

Bath 2: Combine 2 tablespoons each of rosemary and sage, 1 cup of baking soda and 1 cup of sea salt. Mix as before.

Bath 3: This bath simply consists of the herb hyssop. Run your bath water; make it as warm as you desire. Add one cup of hyssop to the water and allow it to steep for several minutes. Swirl your hand in the water and state whatever prayer of protection you desire (I use Psalm 23) a total of 7 times.

No matter which bath you choose, enter the tub (or have the person to be cleansed enter the tub) and begin washing from the top of your (their) head DOWN your (their) body. You know... Its kinda like the old song, "Head, shoulders, knees and toes." It is a common belief in many of the ATROs that to remove a negative influence you move down your body...

Each of these recipes are Spiritual Cleansings that ANY person/practitioner can do. They are simple and can be performed whenever you feel that negativity is rearing its ugly head in your world.

There are times, when baths and smudges aren't even necessary. At these times, simple candle burning rituals may be the key to this. One of my Godmother's favorite things to do was what she called "Warrior's Watch".

The candles you will need for this: St Michael, St George, Guardian Angel, Spell Breaker and, finally, Reversible. You may have to find a local botanica for these, luckily enough, we have a wonderful shop called F & F Botanica (801 N Broad) here in New Orleans where it is VERY easy to acquire the candles necessary for ANY ritual (and they ship, so I can always get hold of them when I am away from Voodoo Authentica on any of the numerous workings I may be out on).

You will also need a picture, possession or representative (such as a doll) of the person you are looking to remove negative intent/energy from.

As always, you will begin this working by calling on Ellegua/Papa Legba

1)   Open the doors by calling/singing/praying to Ellegua/Papa Legba

2)   Pour libations at the door to entice Spirit to join in your working

3)   Light the St Michael candle and pray the St Michael Prayer 1

4)   Place St Michael towards the front of you work space, beginning the formation of a triangle. The first point should be facing toward you, to represent cutting through the negative energy.

5)   Place the representative item of the person to be cleansed from negative intent/energy approximately 6 inches behind St Michael. This is the first step in removing the energy that you, or the person in question, feel(s) that is hampering you/them.

6)   Light the St George candle and recite St George Prayer 2. Place St George behind and to the left of the representative item by 6 inches. This sets up the second level of protective energy to do this work.

7)   Light the Guardian Angel candle and recite Psalm 23. Place the Guardian Angel behind and to the right of the representative item

by 6 inches. This sets up the third level of protective energy to do this work.

8)   Speak words of comfort, peace and protection to the representative item. Say whatever prayer of protection you wish, in this case, I will go with an unknown energy and recite Psalm 85 or 138.

9)   Light the Spell Breaker candle and recite Psalm 7. Place this candle directly to the left of the representative item.

10)   Light the Reversible candle and recite Psalm 145. This Psalm is about the destruction of an enemy (in this case, an unknown jinx/hex/curse).

11)   Allow the candles to burn down naturally (This should take around 7 days. The faster the burn, the better the working).

12)   Close by thanking the Spirits you called on, thanks to God/Olodumare/Bondye for His help in allowing this energy to be removed.

If you remember, I stated that there is even a form of exorcism in New Orleans Voodoo. This ritual MUST be performed by a Voodoo Priest or Priestess however; I will endeavor to explain some of it. This ceremony is done in one of three places. It will either be performed at the Priest's/Priestess' own temple, a lone crossroads or a cemetery.

In preparation of this ritual, a coffin outline will be drawn on the ground in cascarilla and a wet bath will be made. The person who has come to the conclusion that this measure is necessary, will be brought in dressed in regular street clothes. As with ALL ceremonies, Ellegua/Papa Legba will be called on first. Songs and prayers will be sung to Spirits, depending on the House/Family of practitioners (My own uses both the African Orisha and the Haitian Loa) which deal in hex removing/curse breaking/spell removal (the Ghede are said to be the makers and breakers of ALL magick). The person is then laid in the coffin outline. Herbs, oils, incense are used and prayers are spoken over the person. They are stood up and their clothes are ripped and/or cut off of them. The wet bath is brought into play at this point.

Starting at the head, the person is scrubbed downward. Every inch of their body is scrubbed (Men will scrub down a man. Women will scrub down a woman.). When I write "scrubbed" I mean it. It is not like lathering up with a bar of soap. It is, more often than not, not a "gentle" process. Ripping/cutting the clothes off, represents fracturing the magick, while the process of scrubbing is meant to, literally, cleanse the remaining influence off of a person.

The clothes that were removed are gathered up and either burned, buried or left in the cemetery by the, as yet, still naked person. Once this is done, the person is dressed in white, to symbolize their steps into a new, cleaner tomorrow.

The ceremony is closed out as normal.

Personal Note

It is the suggestion of many of the workers that I have had the privilege to come across that you seek out a reputable spiritual worker, should you find that these methods are insufficient. Please, take the time to seek out a REPUTABLE worker, however, bear in mind there is no worker out there that has a "spotless" reputation. This is because, even workers, must answer to the will of God/Olodumare/Bondye. In the end, at the end of a working, if God says "No, this is not for them (at this time)..." then we must bow to it and no amount of work will change this. The second reason you will not find a "spotless" reputation, is that when a worker does magick for someone, they will often give that person specific instructions that they must follow in order to facilitate what they are asking a person to do. Sadly, they never follow through with THEIR end of the working and it causes it to go awry, so, since they don't follow through on their end and do not get what they want, they have decided the WORKER must be at fault. Blame shifting is the new way of life, it seems.

Three Step Spiritual Cleansing

This particular Spiritual Cleansing has been passed down throughout my particular family for four generations that I, personally, know of. It shows just how far back that some things go within the Voodoo community. It also gives an idea of how things adapted to the "New World" and how many subtle shifts that have happened along the progression of Traditions.

This particular Spiritual Cleansing works on more than a few levels. It cleanses the person, inside and out, as well as cleanses and locks

down your home. It is suggested that the home portion of this Spiritual Cleansing be done, at least, once a season, however, you can also do this work ANY TIME you feel as if negative energy or spirits have entered your home.

What you will need to do this:

a gallon bottle of water

24-26 ounces of fine ground sea salt

2 ounces of rosemary

2 ounces of sage

A large mixing bowl

A Bible

Kool aid/lemonade/iced tea

What you are going to do with the first part of this is:

Have the gallon bottle of water blessed by any priest/preacher/minister you trust. Set this aside.

Pour the fine ground sea salt into the large mixing bowl. Begin to mix the salt around with your hands and recite the 23rd Psalm 3 times. Add in the sage, mix it together and recite the 23rd Psalm 2 times. Add in the rosemary and mix the three ingredients. Recite the 23rd Psalm 2 more times then begin to picture safety/sanctuary/protection.

Set aside 1/2 cup of this mixture for later use.

Take the blessed water and mix in any flavor of drink you desire. While mixing, recite the 23rd Psalm 7 times (this is the number of God and there is no one more powerful than God). When you pour the first glass to drink, recite the 23rd Psalm 1 more time (this gives you the number 8 and stands for Spiritual Cleansing). Anyone who drinks of this will find that negativity will be cleansed from INSIDE them.

Take the 1/2 of mixture that I had you set aside and mix it into bath water. While mixing the mixture in the bath water, recite the 23rd Psalm 1 time (again, this gives you the number 8). Bathe in just this water for 20-25 minutes. Step out of the tub, empty it and air dry for 20-25 minutes. Step back in and bathe/shower as you normally would, using all of the soap, shampoo and conditioner you usually would.

With the large, remaining portion of the mixture, you are going to move from room to room of your home and sprinkle a bit of this mixture in each and every corner of EVERY room. In each room, you are going to recite the 23rd Psalm 1 time. This effectively locks the room down. Throw some out each entrance/exit (front door, back door, sliding glass door, garage door) to your home and recite the 23rd Psalm at each…

The Healing Stuff

New Orleans style of Voodoo and, indeed, many of the offshoots of the ATRs carry with them an indigenous amount of healing techniques from herbal to spiritual in nature. Using everything from balms to oils, gris gris to dolls and even herbal concoctions...

Please be VERY aware. If you are allergic to specific ingredients, then it would not do you well to use those ingredients. Take the time to look around and see if items can be traded out... Though some recipes like the first one listed here, should be done according to the recipe for maximum effect, it is always good to use common sense and not go against things you know cause you issues.

Zaar's Four Thieves Vinegar

I've been asked by several people to share this on numerous occasions, and have, on a few occasions done so. I thought I would put it here, for everyone to see one of the things I use to help stabilize my own particular condition...

It is important to note here that I do NOT walk away from Western medicines. I have found a balance between Western medicines and more homeopathic endeavors. Though this recipe does not really have anything to do with Voodoo, it is part of my healing repertoire and as such, I felt here would be a good place for it.

Base: Raw Apple Cider Vinegar (I usually get the largest bottle (1 gallon) which, in turn, will make two batches for me at one ounce "parts" for the dry ingredients)

You will need EQUAL PARTS of these items:

Rosemary, Bay, Lavender, Sage, Thyme, Basil, Jasmine, Mullein, Hyssop and Lemongrass

You will need 1/4-1/2 part (depending on your taste):

Peppermint

You will also need:

8-12 cloves of garlic (I tend to get a little garlic happy and will use 4-6 tablespoons of MINCED garlic)

What you need to do:

Place all herbal ingredients in an air tight container (preferably with a "flip top" lid, but anything air tight will do). Fill the remainder of the container with a half gallon of the raw apple cider vinegar and store in a cool, dark place. Slowly rotate the container every few days to allow the raw apple cider vinegar to permeate all of the ingredients and begin their reaction process.

This becomes active after 2 weeks but for optimal usage, continue the process for 6 weeks.

Strain the herbal ingredients out. These can be used as a poultice for everything from spider bites to sun burn to cuts of various sizes (I **DO** suggest you see a doctor if the issue is severe enough, no matter what the health issue is).

Dosage: 2 tablespoons to 1 ounce in a glass (with honey to taste) by mouth...

I have used this recipe for several years now and am always surprised at the versatility of it. I have used it from everything from the common cold to sore throats to sinus problems to cuts to bruises to sunburns... I'm always finding new things I can use it for or on (in the form of the poultice)...

Healing Oil/Bath 1:

Equal parts oils: peppermint, eucalyptus, rosemary and lemongrass

Dry herbs: peppermint, eucalyptus, rosemary, lemongrass and camphor

Healing Oil/Bath 2:

Equal parts oils: bay, sage, rosemary

Dry herbs: angelica root, lavender and skull cap

Either "Healing Oil" can be used to anoint dolls, candles, gris gris/mojo bags and more. Use the one that best suits your needs.

When using as a bath: Place the ingredients in the tub, fill the tub with warm water, and wash DOWN the body. Remember that Healing is a REMOVAL work

Healing Balm:

This is a healing rub that my grandmother taught me to make to help with my growing pains in my muscles due to my own illness.

What You Will Need:

1 cup of Shea Butter (with more on the side, to aid in thickening)

¼ cup of Cocoa Butter

1 tblspn of Beeswax Pellets

1 tblspn of Palm Oil

1 dram Eucalyptus Oil

1 dram Peppermint Oil

1 dram Camphor Oil

A lidded container large enough to store the mixture.

What To Do:

This recipe can either be done on the stove top or in a microwave safe container so pick the way you would like to do it. Melt down the Shea Butter, Cocoa Butter, Beeswax Pellets, and Palm Oil until it can be mixed together completely. Allow it to cool until it begins to cloud… Mix in the 3 drams of oils and pour into the container allowing it to set overnight.

This rub can be used on your sore muscles and will dull the ache with a nice icy heat. I've been using this rub for several years to my delight. Remember, just because I've used it for years and can take the icy heat doesn't mean that you can, so play around with the mixture. It can always be melted down again and more oils added as necessary.

To make a "healing voodoo doll":

You can generally use any simple doll pattern to create this sort of doll. I generally use a light blue cloth with white stitching for this particular piece of work. Find something to use as a primary filler... This can be anything from indigenous plant life in your area to batting for pillows to anything.

Collect together some herbs that work well with healing energies, such as peppermint, eucalyptus, angelica and lavender. Focus your intent to heal into the herbs and say whatever healing prayer or Psalm you desire as you mix the herbs with your hand.

You will need something to represent the recipient of the healing energies you are sending. Most commonly people will use the name written down on a small piece of paper 9 times however, it is not that uncommon for people to use hair and nail clippings to link the doll to the recipient. Either way works for the purposes here.

A few of the Psalms that I use and what kind of healing I use them for are:

General Physical Healing/ Psalms 3, 19, 89, 102 and 127

Heal From Addiction/ Psalms 101 and 124

Heal A Fever/ Psalms 105 and 106

Heal A Sleeping Disorder/ Psalm 4

Heal A Spiritual Disorder or Emotional Issue/ Psalms 40, 61, 67, 85 and 138

What to do:

-Stitch the doll together leaving the "head" of the doll open. Take your filler and stuff the doll half way, insuring to push some into the legs/feet area of the doll.

-Place some of the healing herbs that you mixed up into the doll (A good tablespoon or two should do the trick nicely).

-Place the recipient identifier in the doll to insure that the person meant to receive the blessing of healing is the one it goes to.

-Add another tablespoon or two full of the healing herbs

-Fill the rest of the way with your choice of filler

-Stitch the head closed and recite any closing prayer or Psalm you have chosen for your work.

Pretty much easy as pie, when you get right down into it.

Healing From a Distance

What you need:

-Picture or candle of the Archangel Raphael

-whole peppermint leaves

-whole eucalyptus leaves

-a light blue 7 day candle

-healing oil

-a voodoo doll to represent your target

-parchment paper

-2 pins with LIGHT BLUE heads on them (these can be found at hobby shops, your local Walmart, and any fabric shop)

-a strip of white cloth 1 foot in length by 2 1 inch in width

What to do:

Anoint the Archangel Raphael and the light blue 7-day candle with the healing oil and set them aside for a few minutes. Write the person's name on the piece of parchment paper 9 times and attach it to the doll with one of the pins. Rub the peppermint and eucalyptus leaves with healing oil while reciting Psalm 89 (a powerful healing

Psalm used in New Orleans Voodoo) and attach them to the doll. Wrap the doll in the white cloth, so that it begins to look like a mummy.

Light the light blue candle and recite Psalm 23 7 times followed by Psalm 89 one time. This will invoke the spirit of God/Olodumare into your healing space.

Light the Archangel Raphael and recite the Raphael prayer. Take the time to state quite clearly EXACTLY who you are trying to heal and what it is you are attempting to heal them from. Remember to speak clearly and concisely, as this is a procedure that requires focus in order to facilitate healing.

A Healing Bath:

What you will need:

-1 cup of fine ground sea salt

-1 cup of Epsom salt

-1 dram Peppermint Oil

-1 dram Eucalyptus Oil

-1 dram Camphor Oil

-3 tablespoons of peppermint

-3 tablespoons of eucalyptus

What to do:

In a large mixing bowl pour both of the salts. Mix them together while reciting Psalm 89 four times. Add the peppermint and eucalyptus herbs and recite Psalm 89 twice more while mixing them into the salts. Add the oils, mix the ingredients together and recite Psalm 89 two final times.

Run a bath (in a pinch a whole pot/bucket of water). Add the mixture to the water. If it is in a bath tub, soak for a few minutes in the mixture and allow it to permeate your being. After a few minutes of soaking, begin to wash DOWN your body. Recite whatever healing prayer you would like at this time. You should bathe this way for at least 20-25 minutes.

Get out of the tub/shower and air dry for 20-25 minutes (as the tub drains).

Return to the tub/shower and bathe as you normally would.

Personal Note

Healing works should NEVER take the place of medical endeavors. They can augment what is already in play.

The Love Stuff

Many of the workings here are collected from various groups, talents and friends I have worked with over the years. Thrown in amongst these things are items of my own creation.

Understand that many of these things will be NON-Spirit oriented however, they can be dedicated to any of the Love entities, such Oshun and Erzulie Freda...

Love workings should be begun on a Wednesday (dedicated to Erzulie Freda) or a Thursday (dedicated to Oshun) and carried on for the length of time necessary to achieve one's goal. Many of the workings should be carried on for no less than 7 days (The time of Creation, 6 days plus the day of rest). Some workings require a bit more dedication, such as the first one listed here...

In the category of love spells there are a whole slew of spell work that can be done. Binding work, break up spells, fidelity/infidelity spells, heartbreak/disappointment spells and so on. I will NOT teach a person how to bind someone NOR will I teach a person how to break up another couple. The rest is fair game. Call me old fashioned, I don't feel like a person should break up another couple just to get with one partner or the other. I also don't believe a person should bind another to themselves. It shows that you aren't willing to allow love to grow through all of its endeavors, taking all of the ups and downs that go with love. Besides... You have to ask yourself... Do you want the person to fall in love with you or the magick that you put out in the universe?

Calling the Qualities

One of the oldest things I can offer in this teaching is one thing I advise on a regular basis to clients who come to me for "love work". "Love work" can be a very tricky thing because, in Voodoo, if done improperly, it will strip a person of their "free will" making them a slave to the magick and not a slave to the love. The first thing I ask a person coming to me to do "love work" is, "do you want him/her to fall in love with YOU or the MAGICK?"

With this working, I will warn you... If the person you have your heart and eyes set on does not hold these qualities anymore, then they will be moved out and a person more matching your listed qualities will be moved into play.

What to do:

First. Take the time to actually write out the list of qualities you desire in your loving relationship. It is the act of physically writing them out that adds a very important element to this working. Do you want the person to be loving, caring, trusting, trustworthy, work as hard as you do to make the bills, spend equal/more time with you as with his/her friends? These are just SOME qualities I listed off to give as example to people who ask, "What do you mean qualities?"

Make a few copies of this list of qualities.

The original copy will be placed in a red school folder and kept, words facing upward, between your mattress and box springs. This is, after all, where you dream of the love of your life.

Get a red or pink novena candle (7 day candle) or a candle dedicated to Oshun, the African Orisha of love, or even Erzulie Freda, the Haitian Loa of love.

Take one copy of the listed qualities and fold it TOWARDS you three times. Place this underneath the candle. Light the candle and recite either Psalm 33 or Psalm 88. Allow the candle to burn for a minimum of 15 minutes. Take longer if you can however, be practical. If you only have 15 minutes a day to dedicate to this, do so. If you do not feel safe leaving a candle burning for the entire time of its capability, then snuff the candle out and go about your business… EACH time you light the candle, recite the Psalm again… It is as simple as that.

Length of time necessary: 21 days

Attraction charm for the Lover's Heart

Here is a little mojo bag that has floated throughout the New Orleans Voodoo community and reportedly created by the Great Mam'selle Marie Laveau.

What you will need:

-parchment paper

-red flannel bag

-pen

-dove's blood ink

-1 teaspoon patchouli

-1 teaspoon lavender

-1 teaspoon powdered vanilla/diced vanilla bean

-1 teaspoon mint (spearmint works best)

-1/2 teaspoon angelica root

-a few drops of Florida Water

-something to burn things in like a small cast iron cauldron, tin can, or the like

On a piece of parchment paper, in dove's blood ink (your blood, menstrual blood or even plain red ink will suffice as well), write the name of your intended lover a total of 7 times.

Recite this "Lover mine through rain or shine, I call to your heart.

If it be the will of God, then we shall never part."

Place the parchment paper and herbs inside your device to burn things. Sprinkle a few drops of Florida Water on the mixture. Stir it around. Add a few more drops of Florida Water and light it with a long stemmed match.

Allow the items to burn together. When they have stopped burning, stir them together again and repeat the above recitation. Put the burned mixture in the red flannel bag and tie it closed.

Carry this mojo bag with you or wear it around your neck. This will draw the one you love closer to you.

"Lover's Heart" (a protective device that can be used to draw love to you as well)

Take a cinnamon stick long enough to carve a name into. Carve the name of your loved one on it on one side of the cinnamon stick and your initials on the other. Use a few drops of "love oil" and "protection oil". Find a red or pink 7-day candle. Light it. Recite Psalm 121 and begin to wrap the cinnamon stick in red yard so that it is completely wrapped. Leave it by the candle until the candle is completely burned down.

Each time that you light the candle you will recite either Psalm 33 or Psalm 88 to draw your lover closer to you and keep them safely in your heart as well as safe in the world around you.

TO BE USED AS A MEANS TO DRAW LOVE: In order to simply draw love to you from an unnamed source you will need to carve the word "love", your initials and the word "communication" on the cinnamon stick. When you light the candle, you will need to recite not only Psalm 121 to begin with but as you continue the work, you will need to recite either Psalm 65 or 67.

REMEMBER!! Magick is practical by nature. If you need to, snuff the candle out and only burn it for certain periods of time do so... With either version of this spell, you should leave the cinnamon stick in place for a period of 7 full days.

Love's Sweet Desire Bath

Dedicated to the Orisha, Oshun, this bath is designed to draw love to a person. This bath is to be done once a week for FIVE weeks. It is suggested that it be done on a Thursday (Oshun's day of the week) however, it can also be done on Wednesday if one is more comfortable working with Erzulie Freda.

What you will need:

-7 red roses

-zest of 5 oranges

-5 drops of honey

-pumpkin seeds

-can of condensed sweetened milk

What you need to do:

Pull the petals off of the roses. Place the ingredients minus the can of condensed sweetened milk in a bath tub and begin running water as warm as you can take over them. Once the bath is full, begin to pour the condensed sweetened milk in the tub and mix it with your hand.

Step into the bath and soak for at least 15 minutes before washing with the water.

Wash going UP your body (feet, calves, knees, thighs, privates/buttocks, stomach, chest, fingers, forearms, elbows, upper arms, shoulders, neck, and head)

Soak until the water is no longer warm.

AIR DRY and wrap your hair.

This bath should be left on your body for one entire day before bathing again.

A Love Work

What you will need:

1 Red or Pink Candle

Psalm 33

5 Red Roses

1 Yellow Rose

1 pair of YOUR dirty underwear

1 pair of HIS dirty underwear

What you need to do:

While reading Psalm 33 aloud, light the red or pink candle. Take the yellow rose and pull the petals from it. Place these petals in HIS underwear. Cut the Red roses from the stem.

As you place each rose flower in HIS underwear, speak CLEARLY, EXACTLY what you are desiring to happen. As you place the last rose in HIS underwear, recite Psalm 33 again.

Wrap up all of these flowers and petals in his underwear. Wrap YOUR underwear around his and tie with a red chord. (Yarn works fine for this, as does red rope) Place this larger package on holy ground (buried if possible. Hidden if not). A temple, shrine, mosque or cemetery.

Leave offerings in the cemetery.

Protective Practices

Here are a few of my favorite protective rituals designed to protect people and their places to live. It is a way to insure that those who outright wish you harm or those that may unintentionally send negative energy to your doorstep are taken care of in the easiest, most reliable fashion.

Household Protections

These are a few of my favorite household protections in the New Orleans Voodoo tradition that are part of my particular family.

At the door:

We, in New Orleans Voodoo, and, in particular, my house will always keep "Warrior Spirits" at the door. In particular, we keep Ellegua, Ogun, and Chango on an altar by our front doors. This accomplishes more than a couple of things. Ellegua, being THE guardian of the crossroads and the opener of pathways (doors) is set to protect the direction and growth of the home in its continuation. Ogun, being the "General", marshals the troops to protect those who live in the home. Chango uses his fire to burn away negative energy, lightning to strike at those who would do you wrong and thunder to warn them when they are beginning to cross the line.

Here's what you do:

On a shelf or table near the front door, begin by cleaning it off with Florida Water and placing a WHITE cloth on it. As you place this cloth on the shelf or table, say a prayer to St Peter, St Michael and Santa Barbara. Follow this prayer by reciting Psalm 23 a total of 7 times. Place an effigy of Ellegua in the center portion of the shelf or table, an effigy of Ogun to the right side of Ellegua, and an effigy of Chango on the left side of Ellegua. In the central section of the shelf or table, in front of Ellegua, place a plate or bowl for offerings to the three Spirits represented on this altar. To the right of Ellegua, in front of Ogun, place a cup for water. To the left of Ellegua, in front of Chango, place a holder for votives.

Every time you approach this altar, knock three times and speak from the heart EXACTLY what you are trying to achieve. Remember to be respectful of these three Spirits guarding your home and, by all means, should you make a bargain with them, as with all members of the Voodoo pantheon of Orisha and Loa, remember to keep it. Ellegua, Ogun, and Chango will protect your home.

Four Corners

What you will need:

1)   4 railroad spikes (these can either be bought off a website like ebay or amazon.com or you can simply walk up and down the railroad tracks [please be safe] and search for discarded spikes. DO NOT DAMAGE RAILROAD TRACKS.

2)   A Bible or Psalm Workbook or book containing the Psalms for Psalms 23 & 121

3)   A gallon bottle of BLESSED water.

What you need to do:

Take the 4 railroad spikes and place them in a mixing bowl. Pour the blessed water on them and recite Psalm 23 a total of 7 times, this brings the power of God/Olodumare/Bondye into the mix. Take the spikes and the rest of the blessed water outside. Go to each corner of your yard and pour some of the remaining blessed water in the corner, pound one of the spikes in each corner and recited Psalm 121.

(if you live in an apartment or have limited yard space, such as here in New Orleans, this can be done in clay pots and placed in the four corners of your home)

Negative Not Allowed.

What You Will Need:

1)   4 silver crosses (the kind you can use to make jewelry with and purchase from Michael's) **2 for each entrance into/out of your home IE front door, back door, sliding glass doors, garage doors**

2)   A container of Holy water.

3)   A Bible, Psalm Workbook or print out of Psalms 23

4)   Glue/Super Glue/Some sort of adhesive

5)   7 ounce bottle of Florida Water

What you need to do:

Calling on the Spirit Ogun (as well as any other Protector Spirits you may wish to) begin outside your FRONT door, and cleanse both sides of the door with the Florida Water. Use the adhesive to attach the crosses on either side of the door, at about eye level. Recite Psalm 23 a total of 7 times for each cross. Move to the back door and repeat the cycle. Move to any other entrance/exit into your home and do the same... This INCLUDES cellar/basement doors.

When you are finished placing all of the crosses on the OUTSIDE of each door way FACING out of your home, recite Psalm 23 one final time. This will actually change the number of all of the crosses from 7 to 8 which, in my lineage, stands for spiritual cleansing, balance, renewal, and healing. It is designed to create a safety bubble around your home.

Protective Gris Gris

What You Will Need:

1)   A swatch of white cloth 4 inches X 4 inches

2)   An 8 inch piece of white chord

3)   1 tablespoon of each: Lavender, Sage, Bay, Rosemary, Rose, Lemongrass, and Peppermint

4)   2 tablespoons olive oil

5)   A bowl to heat all of the herbs and the oil together

6)   A Bible, Psalms Workbook, Psalm 121

What You Need To Do:

Place the herbs in the bowl and mix them together while reciting Psalm 121. Drizzle the oil over them and remix them reciting Psalm 121 again. Stick the mixture in the microwave for 30 seconds. After the microwave goes off, pull the mixture out and place it in the center of your swatch of cloth. Fold up in the fashion as explained in "How to Make a Gris Gris" and tie with the white chord. Recite Psalm 121 one final time and blow on the newly made Gris Gris three times to breathe life into its purpose.

A Protective Bath:

What You Will Need:

1)   A 5 ounce bottle of Kananga Water

2)   2 tablespoons of each: Rosemary, Sage, and Lavender

3)   A Bible, Psalm Workbook, Psalms 23 and 121

4)   A bathtub or bucket/pail/large pot

What You Need To Do:

Run a bath/Fill the pail/large pot with water. Add in the herbs and the Kananga Water. While mixing the herbs and Kananga Water into the regular water, recite Psalm 23 a total of 7 times followed by Psalm 121. As this is a protective bath, you will be drawing the water UP your body.

Remember ANY bath you use that is of POSITIVE benefit must be drawn UP your body.

The Money Magicks

Money is a subject on the minds of millions of people around the world, and Voodoo practitioners are no different. Some of the common things include baths, candle rituals, and calling on specific spirits.

Here are a few of them.

Money Baths

Bath 1:

-1 navel orange sliced navel to stem

-1 package of mint (bruised)

-5 drops of honey

Bath 2:

-the petals of 5 orange roses

-1 navel orange sliced navel to stem

-5 drops of honey

-1 bottle of Florida Water

Bath 3:

-Orange Blossom Cologne

-5 drops of honey

-1 tablespoon of light brown sugar

-1 dram of peppermint oil

-1 navel orange sliced navel to stem

What to do:

Basic Informational piece

All baths are pretty much done in the same style. That is fill the tub, add the ingredients, bathe in the proper direction. Removal of negative energy/spirits is done in a DOWNWARD motion beginning at the top of the head and working down and out towards the toes/bottoms of the feet. Addition of positive energy/spirits is done in an UPWARD motion, beginning at the toes/bottoms of the feet and work up the body to the tops of the head.

Place all the ingredients for the bath in the tub/pocket/bucket that you are going to use. Fill the bath with water as warm as you would like. Begin washing UP your body. This bath is to be done for a total of FIVE days. Each day that you take the bath, focus on the goals you are trying to achieve (IE. Get a job, get a raise, do better on the lottery/bingo, etc.). Work towards these goals and KNOW that the work will help you.

Oshun Offering for Prosperity

What you will need:

-1 pie pumpkin

-5 cinnamon sticks

-1 package light brown sugar

-5 tablespoons ground cinnamon

-the petals of 5 yellow and/or orange roses

-16 ounces of honey

-the closest river to you

What to do:

Open the pie pumpkin by carving off the "cap" like you would when you carve a Jack-O-Lantern and scrape out the insides. Separate out the seeds from the meat of the pumpkin and place them aside. In a bowl mix half of the pumpkin meat, the ground cinnamon, the rose petals, light brown sugar, and honey. While mixing the ingredients, recite Psalm 113.

Once you've completed mixing the items in a bowl, place this mixture back into the pumpkin.

Take each seed, clean it off, speak your wish for prosperity over the seed and drop it into the mixture. Each seed.

Drop in the 5 cinnamon sticks one at a time and recite the Our Father Prayer after each one.

Take the whole preparation to the river and leave it. Make sure to thank God/Olodumare/Bondye, Oshun, and the Ancestors for all their help.

Money Oil 1:

-peppermint oil

-basil oil

-5 drops of cinnamon oil

Money Oil 2:

-bergamot oil

-frangipani oil

-neroli oil

-1/2 portion of peppermint oil

-5 drops of cinnamon oil

Mama Anna Marie's Money Spell

This particular working uses what my Godmother called the "Rue Prayer" (which can be found in the book "Helping Yourself With Selected Prayers [Original Publications] though I will place her version here)

What you will need:

-1 St Peter Candle (white)

-1 St Michael Candle (white)

-5 green votive style candles with holders for each

-5 of each penny, nickel, dime, and quarter

-money oil (pick your flavor)

-Rue water

-the Psalms Workbook

What to do:

Place the two Saint candles to the back of the working.

Light the St Peter candle and recite Psalm 23

Light the St Michael Candle and recite Psalm 113

Place the 5 green votives, in their holders, in front of the two Saint Candles

As you light each candle, place one of each coin in front of it and recite the "Rue Prayer" as follows:

"Beautiful rue, green and fragrant in the world, wherever you are placed in the home you bring fortune and luck.

You bear a secret as no other and never shall you be in need. There is no other in comparison. You free us from all harm and bring the blessings of prosperity and good fortune.

It is for this reason that I beseech your help. I sprinkle your water at my door, for as it is sprinkled, love and money shall enter my home. Amen."

Money for the Business

There are several little "tricks" within the Voodoo traditions that can help with drawing prosperity for a business. Everything from floor washes to candle magicks. I'm going to place some of my favorite ones here.

Floor Wash 1:

-1 dram bergamot oil

-1 dram frangipani oil

-1 7 ounce bottle of Florida Water

Floor Wash 2:

-1 dram peppermint oil

-1 dram basil oil

-1 dram ginger oil

-1 dram cinnamon oil

Floor washes are designed to be used when mopping the floors of an establishment or home-based business and can even be used to scrub down the sidewalks in front of the establishment. My Godmother suggested doing these on a Thursday for the Spirit Oshun since we lived on a the Mississippi River. However, you can do them on a Wednesday for the African Orisha, Oya, if the business is being run by a woman and Friday for the African Orisha, Chango, if the business is being run by a man.

St Expedite Ritual

What you need:

-1 St Expedite statue

-2 green 7 day candles

-amber resin

-fresh peppermint or mint leaves

-2 foot X 2 foot square of gold cloth

-1 saucer, small bowl or cup to use for offerings

-1 shot glass

-spare pocket change

What to do:

Place the square of gold cloth on a table or shelf near the front door of the business. Place the statue of St Expedite in the center of the table or shelf and recite Psalm 23. Place one green candle on either side of St Expedite and the saucer/bowl/cup in front of the statue. Recite Psalm 23 three more times. Place the shot glass on either side of the dish and fill with water. Place mint leaves and amber resin in the bottom of the saucer/bowl/cup and add the change. Recite Psalm 23 one final time.

Once a week, light the candles on either side of St Expedite, allowing them to burn for a while and recite Psalm 23 a total of 5 times. Replace the water, regularly, especially during the weekly ritual reciting of Psalm 23. Add a bit of pocket change at this time.

After the candles burn completely down, use the accumulated pocket change to replace the green candles, mint leaves, and amber resin as necessary.

Each time you replace the mint leaves and amber resin, repeat the Psalm 23 prayers 5 times.

Mama Lola Inspired 7 Fruit Bath

What You Will Need:

1)   7 different fruit items

2)   7 different small bottles of perfumes

3)   A package of fresh of Peppermint and Basil

4)   A gallon bottle of BLESSED water

5)   A blender

6)   A large mixing bowl or bucket

7)   A Bible, Psalms Workbook, Psalms 23 and 49

8)   1 750 ml bottle of rum

What you will need to do:

Peel, slice/cut and place each of the 7 fruits in the blender. Add in the 7 small bottles of perfume. Blend until liquefied (or as smooth as possible) and pour into the mixing bowl or bucket. Add the bottle of rum. While mixing, recite Psalm 23 a total of 5 times, followed by Psalm 49 one time.

Run a bath. Add 1 cup of the mixture to the bath and begin to wash UP your body.

This mixture will last up to 6 months, so make sure to package it securely and use it as often as you would like to draw in extra money to your world.

Made in the USA
Monee, IL
22 June 2024

60111775R10118